A compilation of new material, the book *That Day in September,* and *Huffington Post* blogs

Also by Artie Van Why

That Day in September (2002), a play
That Day in September (2006), a memoir

9/11.

A Survivor's Story.

ARTIE VAN WHY

ISBN: 978-1-4834-8978-0 (sc)
ISBN: 978-1-4834-8980-3 (hc)
ISBN: 978-1-4834-8979-7 (e)

Library of Congress Control Number: 2018909684

Lulu Publishing Services rev. date: 8/21/2018

With much thanks to Stephanie Van Deusen.

Dedicated to:

my mom
(October 18, 1931–April 13, 2017)

and

my dad
(August 2, 1929–December 2, 2017)

Praise for *That Day in September*

The Play

"Van Why's recollections of the attacks and their aftermath are harrowing, marked by an eyewitness perspective that has the sober authenticity of diary entries. **Countless heroes emerged from the chaos of Sept. 11, and by selflessly sharing his story, Van Why must be counted among their number.**"

—David C. Nichols, *Los Angeles Times*

The Memoir

"**Let me just say that this is a flawless memoir.** [I]t so vividly and poignantly captures what it was like to live through that day … Flawless because it is written from the heart."

—Bev Hankins, *My Reader's Block*

"Artie's book is not a book to read and then add to the bookshelf. **It is a book that begs to be passed from hand to hand** so that all of us can know what the people who were there in the midst of the chaos felt and still struggle with. **It is a book of remembrance for a tragedy that we, as Americans, should never forget.**"

—Donna McBroom-Theriot, *My Life. One Story at a Time*

"**This is an incredibly moving, vivid and personal description of one man's experience on the ground on 9/11.** … Van Why brings the reader into his heart and mind that day and the days that followed."

—Julie Bertolini, *My Book Retreat*

Contents

The Blogs

Preface

This book tells you my story of being an eyewitness and survivor of the terrorist attack on the World Trade Center on 9/11. It is also the story of how I came to be there. I share with you some personal aspects of my life before and after moving to New York because when you read about me standing in front of the burning towers, I want you to know the person I was that day— what I had been through, what I had endured, what I had overcome. I don't want to be just a nameless survivor you know nothing about. I want you to understand the past that was then affected by that day.

I then share with you just what I witnessed the morning of 9/11, giving you a glimpse into the sights, sounds, smells, and emotions of that day. I then hope to convey to you what it was like to live in New York City the weeks and months following.

Finally, in what were originally *Huffington Post* blogs, I share with you my life since 9/11—how it dramatically changed, what it is like living with post-traumatic stress disorder (PTSD), depression, anxiety, and all the other manifestations of grief, mourning, and sadness that can be applied to any life-altering experience. It's a section that anyone who has lived through trauma or tragedy might be able to relate to and perhaps find some help in.

Introduction

This book is for anyone who has experienced loss, a broken life, or a horrific, traumatic, or tragic moment in life.

This is not just for eyewitnesses or survivors of 9/11. There are far too many atrocities and sorrows in this world that people have witnessed and lived through besides 9/11. Some stories are very public; some are very personal.

No matter what upheaval befalls you, we all are then faced with what seems so impossible—continuing with our lives. I don't have the answer as to how we do that. I am still learning and am sharing with you what I have discovered.

> You're always one decision away from a totally different life.
> —Mark Batterson

"The Forgotten Majority"

When people think of 9/11 (particularly as each anniversary approaches), they automatically think of the people who died that day. That is how it should be. Those are the ones we want to never forget.

Our thoughts turn to the families that lost a loved one. The people who lost a friend. The companies that lost coworkers. We acknowledge their continuing grief.

We remember, too, the heroes in public service who died that morning in the line of duty, doing what they had been trained for. The firefighters, the New York Police Department and Port Authority police, the EMS and EMT workers. The World Trade Center facility personnel and Port Authority engineers who stayed behind to help rescue people. And the private civilians who ran into the towers to offer their aid.

These are the people who can't be ignored or forgotten. Nor can we forget the victims at the Pentagon or the heroic passengers of Flight 93.

However, there is a group of individuals who probably don't cross people's minds when they remember 9/11 and, specifically, the attack on the World Trade Center. This group is not thought of or acknowledged publicly on the anniversaries.

I am part of this group, and we number in the thousands. I refer to us as "the forgotten majority." We are the innocent bystanders who were in the streets that morning. The multitude of people who surrounded the World Trade Center. The ones who just happened to be there that day.

We are the office workers evacuated from our buildings and thrust out onto those streets.

The tourists who were there to see the Twin Towers.

The bicycle messengers.

The news vendors who sold us our daily newspaper at their stands.

The people manning the silver coffee carts on the street corners.

The people who usually weren't there daily but, for whatever reason, just so happened to be in the wrong place at the wrong time that day.

We were mere civilians, finding ourselves on the front line of a battlefield, bereft of any basic training.

We are the living eyewitnesses. We are the 9/11 survivors.

Somehow, we survived that morning, but we feel abandoned by the public.

For the most part, people aren't aware that many of us still struggle with survivor's guilt, fueled with the question of why we survived and the others didn't. Many, like myself, wish at times that we hadn't survived. I and many other 9/11 survivors suffer from PTSD.

Like me, some of us are still in therapy, grappling with finding our place in this world now that the life we once had is gone. Some deal with their inner demons alone, talking to no one.

We are now spread all over the globe, so many of us, myself included, having moved away from New York City. We now live in places where there are no other ex–New Yorkers who were there in the city on 9/11. Though we may have left the city we loved, the nightmares, flashbacks, images, anxieties, depression, and phobias didn't stay behind. They remain with us to this day. And, like strangers in a strange land, we have no one who can relate to our experiences or emotions.

When I left New York and moved to Lancaster, Pennsylvania, in 2003, if I told people I was from NYC, some would ask if I was there on 9/11. When I answered in the affirmative, telling them I was standing in front of the Twin Towers, they would get a look of panic in their eyes as if they didn't know how to respond to that. They didn't expect that precise of an answer. To ease their obvious discomfort, I usually changed the subject. It got to the point where I would try to avoid mentioning I was a 9/11 survivor just so other people wouldn't feel ill at ease.

What I longed for, though, was for someone who found out I was a survivor to ask me questions. I wanted someone to not be afraid to ask, "Oh my God, what was that like? Do you mind my asking?" No, I wouldn't have minded at all. I needed to talk about it. To share my story. Instead, it stayed silently within during my first few years in this new place I was trying to establish as home.

Many of us survivors are connected through a private support group on Facebook. Only another survivor can truly understand what others of us go through. The loneliness. The constant sadness. The mental anguish. The unspoken cries for help. We are more than friends. We are united with one another. People I've never even met face to face have helped me. Our relationships of support are built on emails, private messages and posts on Facebook, and occasional phone calls.

If you can, think about us on the next anniversary. As you mourn the physical deaths of the innocent, remember the spiritual, psychological, and emotional deaths of the survivors.

Those who died take precedence—without question.

But if you personally know a survivor of 9/11, think of taking a moment to simply ask how he or she is doing as the anniversary nears.

Maybe tell that person you're there if he or she needs to talk.

If it seems comfortable and right, a gentle hug and "I'm thinking of you" could make all the difference. Or a card or email. A phone call. An act of kindness that lets the survivor know he or she is not forgotten.

Life Questions

I've wrestled inwardly for years over the questions that come with trying to make sense out of my existence. Is fate a real factor in how my life has played out? Is there such a thing as a specific plan for one's life, and if so, who's the mastermind behind it? God? The universe? Karma? Luck?

Is there validity to the adage "Everything happens for a reason"? Or are things that happen to us "just meant to be," as some suggest?

Spiritually speaking, if a God does control everything that happens, wouldn't that reduce God to a puppeteer, manipulating our lives and making us mere puppets?

I've come to believe, for now, that we control our destiny, which, in turn, determines our fate. Our control thrives by the decisions we make throughout our lifetimes. I think back over my own life and see how the decisions I've made (the good ones, the questionable ones, and the extremely bad ones) shaped the directions my life took with every hurdle, valley, hill, or mountain I encountered. We always face crossroads in life where we must decide to either turn left or turn right. Or, just stay still, stuck because of an inability to decide.

When I graduated from college in 1976, I was stuck. I had no clue as to what I wanted to do with my life or what my next step should be. So, I went back to my hometown of Gaithersburg, Maryland to live with my parents for a year after graduation, and I worked for a pharmaceutical company, in the shipping department—that is until fate, or whatever one wants to call it, stepped in and ultimately led to me becoming a 9/11 survivor.

In November 1977, I visited New York for the first time. I didn't expect to be presented with any opportunity to stay there, but, through a rare set of circumstances, I was given the chance to move there to act in a play. All I had to do was say yes. Did that decision to say yes to the opportunity, now so much a part of my history, take me one step closer to being on Church Street in front of the World Trade Center on 9/11? If my decision had been "no," would I even be writing this book? Maybe not. But allow me to backtrack to how I ended up in New York in November 1977 and how I made that first of what would be quite a few life-changing decisions.

In My Beginning ...

In June 1976, I graduated from a small, conservative evangelical Christian college in Kentucky. Going there required me to make some drastic changes in my way of living. I had to have my shoulder-length hair cut above the ears. I couldn't wear my standard attire—blue jeans and T-shirts—to class. There were the other standard prohibitions most Christian colleges and universities had during that time: no drinking, swearing, smoking, or dancing; no dresses above the knee; and certainly no public displays of affection.

Why would I put myself in such a restrictive, rigid environment? you might ask. I was a child of the "Jesus movement" (an evangelical Christian movement of the early 1970s among young people), and I believed God wanted me to go there. More about that later.

During my senior year of high school, I became a born-again Christian, with a bit of Evangelicalism, Fundamentalism, and Pentecostalism thrown in the mix—meaning I thought if you didn't believe in Jesus, you were going to hell. I took the Bible literally and partook in the "gifts of the spirit" (speaking in tongues, delivering prophecies, laying on of hands for healing). I was also very naïve and lost, as most teens usually are. What drew me to God was a dynamic youth leader whose personal attention made me believe I mattered. When he told me that God loved me and had a specific plan for my life, I embraced that concept. Being a "lost teen," I interpreted that to mean I wouldn't have to make any big decisions, such as what to do with my life. God would tell me. So, you can see I shied away from decision making early on.

It was also during my senior year that I became aware that I was gay. I knew, even as a child, that I was different, that I was drawn to other boys. I was struck with *bromances* way before that was even a word. I didn't like what most preteen boys did, like baseball and football or sports in general.

Sports were the furthest things from my mind. But I would play along with those reindeer games to prove to others, and to myself I guess, that I was just like everyone else. Only I wasn't. When I was a senior, I realized the word for this "difference" I felt: *homosexual*.

Religion aside, from my limited exposure to social norms, I had gathered that being gay was considered, at that time, not normal. Early on, some primal instinct told me that I had to hide and not talk about my attraction to boys. At an early age, I began to believe this interest in boys made me a bad person. Thinking I must be the only one who felt this way, I assumed I had something terribly wrong with me.

My involvement with God came along at the right time to confirm that assumption. Along with my conversion to Christianity came the message early on that God thought homosexuality was a sin. An abomination, to be precise, that would send me to hell. Tell that to an impressionable, confused kid, and it scared me straight. Or, rather, it scared me enough to start praying for God to make me straight. And I prayed relentlessly for that to happen. I wanted to believe that God could "fix" me and make me normal.

To show God I was serious, I committed to do with my life whatever God wanted. I would give up my attraction to other males, and my lifelong ambition of becoming a star of stage and screen.

Ever since I can remember, I wanted to be an actor when I grew up. I would put on little shows with my cousin when we were children for our mothers to watch (the fathers were noticeably not interested in these musical extravaganzas I would come up with). I bought cast albums without even really knowing what the shows were about, but I'd learn the lyrics and sing in my bedroom. And when *The Ed Sullivan Show* had a number performed from the latest Broadway hit, it mesmerized me.

I became active in school plays starting in elementary school and continuing through high school. My mom was the one who would come see me in them. But her attendance didn't mean she approved. Both she and my dad discouraged me in wanting to pursue something so frivolous. I heard "you can't" almost as a mantra when growing up. When I asked if I could take dancing lessons, I was told by my mother, "boys don't do that" (a variation of "you can't"). I got the same response from her when I asked if I could take piano lessons.

If my own parents didn't want me to become an actor, would God? I decided to let God decide for me. There was only one school I really wanted to go to after high school: North Carolina School of the Arts. It was the only college I applied to (much to my parents' dismay). I flew down to the school to audition, which was part of the application process.

To be honest, I was so scared and unsure of myself, I don't think I made a favorable impression on the audition committee.

My intuition proved right. I can still remember it as if it were yesterday, when I stopped at home one day after school on my way to a Bible study at a neighbor's house. There, I found a letter from the School of the Arts, and it wasn't one of acceptance; the school didn't want me. I can still feel the disappointment now.

I went to the Bible study, and during the study, I determined the rejection letter was God's way of telling me I shouldn't become an actor.

So, I couldn't be attracted to who I was drawn to—boys—and I couldn't do what I loved to do—act. God was taking away the two profound parts of who I was. Though I didn't consciously acknowledge the thought, this planted the seed in me that everything about me was bad and God was a very mean-spirited figure who would say "no" a lot (variations of what I'd hear from my parents). God was a god of "you can't." And I thought God was supposed to be one of love.

I believed I could no longer follow, or have, anything that I wanted or dreamed of, especially if I wanted it for seemingly selfish reasons. I was misguided to believe I had to give up anything that made me happy or that was part of my genetic makeup. I convinced myself that "serving God" was enough and that would make me happy.

By now, I was caught up in this new faith I had voluntarily committed myself to. I just accepted that what I wanted wasn't God's will. So, I now prayed to not be gay and for God to take away my love for acting. I left it up to God to show me what to do. I handed over that decision to divine guidance.

Having had no backup plan for college, I lived with my parents the year after graduating from high school and worked at a factory that made air-conditioning units for computer rooms. I carried my little black pocket-sized Bible in my blue jeans back pocket. I think I was trying to convince my coworkers, and God as well, that I was a devout Christian man, as I read through it at lunchtime.

I started looking at other colleges and found out about one in Kentucky that had a reputation for being one of the finer Christian colleges. I applied and was accepted, so, in my mind, that was God putting me where I was supposed to go. The school had a drama department and a drama major, but I assumed that if I was to serve God, I should put aside all thoughts of becoming an actor and enter my freshman year as a Bible major, with the sincere intention of trying to please God.

I'd say my first two years in college were years of living in denial and suppression, and forsaking my attraction to men and to acting, believing God had taken away both of those desires. I was a lousy Bible student, and I didn't date. But when my junior year came, bam! I realized I was still attracted to men and I still wanted to be an actor. Despite all my praying, God hadn't taken away my gayness and hadn't sparked a true desire within me to want to study the Bible.

I was forced to face these two things about myself at last. God hadn't fixed me, and I began to grow resentment that turned to anger toward God. I stopped wanting to be a servant of God, as I realized my feelings of wanting to be an actor had never really gone away. I had just boxed them up and put them on a shelf.

So, what was I to do with all this self-awareness? Something had to change. Something had to be done. After much turmoil, thought, prayer, and meditation, I "came out." I declared myself a drama major. I decided to keep quiet, celibate, and closeted about my sexual orientation. And I began to earnestly beg this God I was angry with (yet professed to love, out of fear) to take away my attraction to men.

At least I could be open about my desire to act. Since I was the only drama major in the class of '76, I became a big fish in our very small pond of a drama department. A drama department where all scripts had to be reviewed, edited, and approved before being presented, and where, though we put on musicals, we did them, of course, without the choreography. No dancing, remember? It was not the best of institutes to learn the craft of acting. It was no North Carolina School of the Arts!

As to my sexual identity, I replaced what I know now was my natural orientation with the façade of heterosexuality, which planted the seed of self-loathing. I now pleaded with God to make me straight. But those pleas went unheard, or so it seemed. My resentment toward God grew. During my last two years of college, I never talked to anyone about the inner turmoil I was going through. Not even my roommate and best friend. No one asked, so I didn't tell. I mistakenly always thought I was the only one on campus with this personal struggle over sexual orientation. It wasn't till years later I found out that really wasn't true. If only I had known that then. I also have discovered that back then, if there was even a suggestion of a student being gay, that student would suddenly no longer be enrolled at the college.

After College

I graduated from college angry at the school and the atmosphere that permeated the college, which suggested that we had to be perfect Christians (or pretend to be) while keeping our individual secrets, which were proof of us all being flawed human beings.

And I graduated angry at God for not "fixing" me. Yet I was also deathly afraid of God's judgment and the idea that I was destined for hell. I wanted nothing to do with God yet felt too frightened to push God out of my life. My spiritual belief in God became one based on anxiety, despair, and fear.

I took this internal conflict with me when I went to live with my parents after graduation. I hadn't received the direction I expected God to give me as to what I should do with my life after college. So, living with my parents till I could figure that out was my only solution. I had a college degree yet was working at a pharmaceutical company.

I kept up the pretense of being straight. I did my best not to be asked, and not to tell, if I was gay, thinking if I ignored it, my sexual orientation would go away either by my sheer determination or by God finally deciding to respond to my pleas. As afraid as I had been of my college finding out my secret, I was now scared of my parents finding out. So, the secret continued being just that.

I distracted myself from my inner turmoil by following my love of acting (or of getting outside attention and approval) and doing community theater. Other than that, I had no set plans or goals. I was stuck and afraid of approaching any crossroads that would cause me to have to decide.

But I don't give myself enough credit. Each time I auditioned for a role, I had made the decision to do so. And it was at one of those auditions where my dream of a "big break" came to fruition. That happened when I auditioned for, and was cast in, the title role of a professional dinner theater production of *Norman ... Is That You?* in Greensboro, North Carolina (a comedy about a young gay man who's terrified to come out of the closet). Art imitating my life?

I gladly left the pharmaceutical business to finally become a professional actor. It was because of that decision to audition for that play that I ended up in New York in November 1977. Therefore, the act of making decisions fascinates me. Though a decision may seem like a simple one, the ripples that fan out from it can push our lives outward to experiences we never would have imagined. If I hadn't been cast as Norman in that play, I wouldn't have met the person who would become the catalyst who got me to New York.

During the run of *Norman … Is That You?* I developed a close friendship with one of the women in the show. I'll call her *Karen*.

Having had no substantial emotional ties (or physical ties or sexual ties or any other kind of ties) with any woman up till that time, I jumped—no, I grabbed—onto the idea that I was in love with Karen and therefore couldn't be gay. (I didn't realize then that there are many kinds of love.) My love for Karen was genuine, but I mistook my feelings for Karen for romantic love, believing that God had finally answered my prayers and I was now straight. What I was was naïve. It took me quite a while to figure out my love for Karen was a love of friendship, whereas Karen's love for me was blossoming romantically.

Since our relationship had begun as a friendship, I had confessed to Karen that I was gay but didn't want to be. Karen also had a confession. She had a boyfriend in New York. So as our friendship evolved into a relationship, it was based on both of us having a secret. Our love for each other grew, yet unconsciously in different directions and, unintentionally, for different reasons.

Getting to New York

When the final week of performances of *Norman ... Is That You?* was over the week before Thanksgiving of 1977, I drove Karen up to New York. She needed to get there because she was subletting a friend's apartment. Plus, she needed to face her boyfriend with the truth of what had transpired between her and me. To put it bluntly, she was going to decide whether she wanted to remain with him or she wanted to be with me—door number 1 or door number 2.

I was going to stay with Karen in her New York sublet for two days of sightseeing, since I'd never been to the city before, and then I would drive back to my parents' home and wait out Karen's decision. Instead of God, I was letting Karen decide my fate.

We drove in on the New Jersey Turnpike on a Monday night. Seeing the skyline of Manhattan for the first time was like discovering the Emerald City. And there, standing majestically above all the other buildings, were the Twin Towers of the World Trade Center.

My excitement was tangible. I could hardly believe I was about to drive into the city that had always been part of my childhood and adult dream. It was a magical moment for me and was about to start the newest chapter in the story of my life.

We stayed overnight in the studio apartment Karen had sublet. The plan was I would stay for two days and head back to Maryland on Thursday, in time for Thanksgiving. Karen's boyfriend didn't know she was in the city. The pattern of secrets and lies continued.

I can't even tell you what we did that next morning and afternoon. But there's no forgetting what took place that evening. I saw my first Broadway show: *A Chorus Line*. And what an introduction to Broadway! Yet another magical moment. As the cast sang, "God, I hope I get it," I sat there, in awe, wanting it too, whatever it was.

On Wednesday, we planned to go see Liza Minnelli in *The Act* in the afternoon. That was my choice. I think the dam that, unbeknownst to me, was holding back my truth that I was a gay man was beginning to crack. I chose Liza Minnelli, in all her spangled glory, over any other Broadway offering, or a romantic walk in Central Park with Karen.

Before seeing the matinee, I had something I wanted us to do. Somehow, I had ended up on the mailing list of a Christian theater company, housed in a church right off Times Square on Forty-Forth Street. I wanted to find this church and find out more about the theater company. At that time, I couldn't remember just where it was, except somewhere in the Forties off Times Square. Karen and I walked up and down every street in the Forties but couldn't find the building. Just as we were about to give up, while walking west on Forty-Forth Street, Karen spotted it.

We walked into the lobby of what was once the famous Lambs Club, which, in its heyday, was a social club for actors, songwriters, and others involved in show business (particularly theater folk). As we entered the building, I went up to the reception desk and asked the girl sitting there if I could get some information about the Christian theater group. She pointed to a guy across the lobby who had his back to us. She suggested I go talk to him because he was part of the group.

I went over to him and tapped him on the shoulder, saying, "Excuse me." He turned around, and lo and behold, he was someone I knew from college. We both were at a loss for words initially. What a small world that big city could be at times.

He asked me what I was doing there, and I said I wanted information about the theater group. Then he said words that would change my life. "You're not going to believe this," he said. "We're in rehearsals for our Christmas show, and one of the actors dropped out today. I was just with the director, and we prayed that a Christian actor would walk through these doors today!"

Divine Intervention?

I still, after all these years, don't know what to make of that life-changing encounter. My college acquaintance took me to meet with the director. We talked for a while. Then the director offered me the job and asked if I could be back in New York for rehearsals on Friday. I said yes, of course.

So, was that divine intervention? Or an example of being in the right place at the right time? Luck? Karma? Pure coincidence? Or something that just happened?

I have no idea how to answer those questions even these many years later. But back then, at that moment, I believed it was God's intervention, part of that wonderful plan God had for my life, which was what drew me into a life of faith to begin with. In that moment, I believed (in astonishment) that this was God at work in my life. And I took it to mean that God was telling me that it was okay to be an actor and that I was to move to New York.

If I'd never walked into that building, who knows what my outcome would have been. Would I still have ended up living in New York City and become a 9/11 survivor? For sure, it forced Karen to decide between me and the boyfriend, since I would come back to the city in a few days. She would deal with that decision when I drove back to Maryland (after seeing Liza, of course).

My parents seemed in shock when I showed up back home with my news and asked them to sell my car. But I packed my bags and took the train back up to my new home! For my first year in New York, every time I talked on the phone with my folks, my mom would always ask, "So when are you coming home?" It took awhile for it to sink in with her that New York was now my home.

So, back in Manhattan, I was ready to start my new career as a New York actor. I fell right into rehearsals, and in a matter of weeks, I made my New York debut working a very large puppet on a stick in a children's Christmas play about the nativity story. It might not seem like much of a show-business break, but I was performing on a New York stage at the Lamb's Theatre (a beautiful small theater that famous performers once used back when it was the Lambs Club).

Karen broke up with the boyfriend, and she and I lived in the studio sublet, which was down in the West Village. However, my ideal dream come true was about to be challenged. During the '70s, the West Village was the mecca for the gay community. That's where most of the gay bars and the gay-owned shops and boutiques were. Just walking to the corner deli for a cup of coffee, I'd pass more gay men and women than I had ever seen in my life. It seemed like there were herds of them all throughout the Village. And that's not counting the gay men I met now that I was auditioning for shows.

Suddenly, that assuredness I had that Karen was the answer to my prayers and that I could be straight wasn't so assuring. Taking in the whole of the gay community, I realized that I wasn't an oddity. The crack in that dam holding back my natural sexual orientation was widening. And I used guilt to fill that crack.

I felt torn up inside. Here, I believed God had brought me to New York, and there I was, having these sinful desires for other men. Was that any way to repay God? And, of course, I kept all of this to myself. I didn't dare share it with Karen. Or anyone. This was the beginning of what would be years of struggling between my sexuality and my spirituality. Since that old Lamb's building was now owned by a church (which held Sunday services in the theater), I became part of a faith community almost by no choice. I was no longer pure in heart, as I would sit through church services constantly reminded of what a sinner I was.

I sat on the fence, with one foot on the side of God and keeping my salvation and the other foot on the side of starting to explore the gay part of me. I acted unfaithfully by having clandestine encounters with men, so I was once again living in secrecy, afraid of Karen or anyone finding out. And, knowing I couldn't keep this a secret from God drove me into the beginning of depression, which would destructively deepen.

I was so filled with guilt. I berated myself for being such a bad person. After any physical encounter with another man, I would pray to God, pleading for forgiveness and promising that I would never be with a man again. Of course, that promise didn't last. It became a ridiculous cycle of secretly going out to explore gay life, then praying a promise to God I'd never do it again. Those promises never lasted, and now, I was letting God down. I would surely go to hell to pay for it.

If you're reading this and wondering, yes, the inevitable did happen. Karen went away to do a show, and while she was gone, my illicit encounters turned into me having a summer affair with a man in her absence.

The Depth of Depression

When Karen came back from her show, I had to do the right thing and tell her what had happened while she was gone. Once I told her, she reached for her Bible, and we swore to one another and God that we would work through this together. Though I tried to be faithful, the affair continued. Like with so many other Christian gay men who have tried to live two lives, my depression intensified. I tried all I could to make myself straight. Attending ex-gay ministries, counseling with pastors, spending time at a monastery—none of it worked.

I fell so deep into clinical depression that I contemplated suicide. That scared me, so for my life's sake, I entered a psychiatric hospital for a month. It was there that the words of a therapist gave me the courage to take the first baby step toward being myself, believing that God created me as I was, sexual orientation included.

During one of our therapy sessions, I asked my therapist, "Why isn't God answering my prayers?"

He replied, "Maybe you're praying the wrong prayers. Maybe you should be praying for God to help you accept yourself for who you are."

That was my aha moment. But it by no means suddenly unburdened me of all the shame, guilt, fear, and self-loathing. It was a baby step. A very small baby step. It took many years for me to claim the truth of who I was spiritually, emotionally, psychologically, mentally, and sexually. They were difficult years, and I am saving those years and stories for another book someday.

I was in my thirties when I slowly opened the closet I had kept myself in for so long. I lost all my friends from the Christian community at the Lamb's when I came out to them because, to them, I was an unrepentant sinner. As one of the leaders of an ex-gay ministry I was part of told me over the phone,

"I'll watch you burning in the fires of hell." Those were her last words before hanging up on me.

Reactions like that made me feel I had to make a choice between God and an authentic life. So, I walked away from any form of a life of faith for the longest time.

As for my coming-out process, I decided to take the biggest, and most courageous, step I'd ever taken. I made a special trip to Maryland one weekend to see my folks and tell them what I felt they needed to know. That weekend, I came out to them, telling them I was gay. Their initial response was that I was their son and they would always love me. Not every young gay man or woman is granted that unconditional acceptance. Nothing much else was said that night. It was late, and we went to bed.

The next morning, I woke up and went into the kitchen, where my mom was. The stairs to our basement were right off the kitchen, and I could hear my dad down there, crying. My mother said I should go down to him, so I did. I stood there, his back to me, him still in tears. When he sensed I was there, he came over to me, sobbing, and said, "This is hard for me. I'm going to need time, but I love you." He then embraced me. That was the first time my father had ever hugged me. I finally felt validated as a person.

Jump ahead many decades, and my dad would be the first to bring up the latest news affecting the gay community. He and my mom even posed with me for a photo that went on a billboard during Gay Pride, celebrating the diversity of families. It took time, but he did, indeed, change with the times. I saw him grow in many ways. He became a role model, having recognized his personal imperfections and worked to change them, becoming a man of depth—the kind of dad a son would hope to emulate one day.

You may be wondering whatever became of Karen. She is married with four beautiful daughters and a loving husband, and she is still involved in theater as a Broadway producer. Perhaps none of that would have happened for her if she hadn't spent those unsettling years with me.

That brings up yet more unanswerable questions for me. Are people brought into our lives or we into theirs for a reason? Is that just a roll of the dice? Happenstance? Or do our connections with one another as human beings occur to serve a greater good? Or to push our lives in another direction?

The Dream Becomes a Nightmare

You already know what my beginning years in New York were like. During all the inner, and outer, turmoil I went through, I was trying to pursue an acting career that I thought awaited me in the Big Apple. I auditioned for shows but would be lucky if I got a callback. I'm sure that my self-loathing, guilt, and shame must have affected how I came across to those I auditioned for.

I probably wore my assumed unworthiness as an outer skin when auditioning in front of people. I had lived with my guard up constantly because I needed a wall to hide behind. I could never truly reveal the real me to others.

I believed that God wasn't happy with me. God had miraculously given me the opportunity to move to New York to act, I thought. And I repaid God by breaking Karen's heart and living a sinful life as a gay man. Why should God reward that? In my warped thinking, I believed God wasn't letting me land acting jobs as a wrathful punishment (from a vengeful God). Even as I write this, it all sounds so conflicted and absurd and pretty much self-centered. I had the audacity to think the God of the universe had nothing better to attend to than making sure I didn't get a role in a show.

The few shows I did do were mostly in some way associated with Karen. This made me feel inadequate and certainly didn't help my already low self-esteem.

By the time 1988 rolled around, I had to admit that a successful acting career wasn't in the cards for me. And to be perfectly honest, I think I was more interested in being famous than being a serious actor. I'm sure that all stemmed from those feelings of being different as a child—the old "I'll show everyone I'm somebody" logic. I couldn't have cared less about Shakespeare. I wanted stardom.

As do most struggling actors, I would have to take on "survival" jobs in between theater jobs. I learned the trade of word processing when computers were just starting to be used in the business world. It was the one talent I knew I had. So, I figured I would take a break from my meager acting career and get a "real" job. I went to an employment agency.

My first interview I was sent out on was to work as an evening word processor for a midsize law firm in Midtown Manhattan. By the time I got back to my apartment, the agency had left a message on my answering machine saying that the firm wanted to hire me. So, I didn't even have to have a callback. I made the audition. I was now a working member of the corporate world, with a steady paycheck, benefits, and paid vacations. I accepted the job, promising myself that it would only be for a year or two. I would get some money in the bank and then go back to my acting career or decide on something else to do.

Since it wasn't a huge firm, it only had one word processor who worked from nine to five and me, with my shift from five to midnight. Those hours suited me just fine. My shift ended when the nightlife was just beginning among theater folk, which included most of my good friends. We'd usually meet each night at one of the neighborhood watering holes.

I didn't really start drinking till my midtwenties. I was a lightweight drinker. One or two beers was all I could handle. And I stayed away from the hard stuff.

All of that would change. And not for the better.

A New Secret to Keep

When one makes it a practice to meet at a bar night after night, drink after drink, one's tolerance to booze slowly begins to build up. For me, one or two beers soon became ten or more. The hard stuff wasn't so hard to swallow after all, meaning I'd drink just about anything put in front of me if alcohol was in it. And, after a while, I'd willingly partake of any drugs offered by anyone anywhere.

Since New York bars didn't close till 4:00 a.m., my evenings turned into early mornings, as I'd stay out till that very last "last call" was shouted out. Then there were the after-hours haunts I would sometimes go to after my friends and I parted ways for the evening. I assumed they knew nothing of this other side of me, the one that led me to stay out past 4:00 a.m., drinking or partying wherever I could find a party.

My drinking and partying got out of hand even though I thought that I had it all under control and that my friends weren't aware of what I'd do once we separated at night. I found myself living another secret life, as I had with my sexuality all those years ago.

Growing up, I had sworn that I would never drink. Excessive drinking was prevalent on both sides of my family. I knew what alcoholism looked like and smelled like. And I saw the Jekyll-and-Hyde effect it could have, turning a pleasant person into a domineering bully. So, I swore that would never happen to me.

But unfortunately, my DNA had the disease of alcoholism marked deeply within it, just waiting for me to set it in motion. Those one or two drinks a night opened a Pandora's box that complicated my life until I had no control over it. I got caught up in a whirlpool of excess and addiction.

I was what you could call a *happy drunk*. Not a mean bone was present when I drank. I was the "drinks for everybody" type of guy. I also was a blackout drunk. Countless mornings, waking up, I had no idea how I had gotten home, or what I had done the night before. I shudder now when I think of the situations I allowed myself to be put into and don't want to even imagine any situations I cannot remember.

I'm sure I'm not the only person who has realized I was not living the life I thought I would. Most of my adult life, I was a man without a plan. I'd go in the direction circumstances would take me, thinking I had few other options. I didn't have God to rely on anymore.

I was working at a job that I had never considered as a career choice. But I felt too comfortable with the positives of a steady job, good pay and benefits, vacation days, a 401(k) plan—all the trappings of success.

I was afraid to think ahead to the future because I had no plans—no alternative to this life I was living. I figured I'd remain at my job the rest of my life. I seemed to destruct any potential relationship I was in, so I feared growing into a lonely old gay man, living all by myself, stuck in a no-win job till I'd retire. It depressed the hell out of me.

I was at rock bottom, at the bottom of a deep hole, and looking up, I could barely see the sun shine. I wanted to call out to God to help me, but I'd walked away from all that.

I wanted someone to come along who would make everything all right again. I wanted someone to save me from myself. Yes, I was at rock bottom, and it was pretty deep, pretty dangerous, and not very pretty. In the grand scheme of things, though, that was where I had to be before help would arrive.

There comes a time for some of us, I guess, when the subtle awareness of the question "How did I get here?" grows into a harsh reality. At one time, I had wanted more out of life. The hope I tried to hold on to was the false hope that my life would change on its own. Somewhere, there would be a right place to be at the right time where I'd run into the right person who would magically change my life. So, pour me a drink, and let me complain about what could have been. Pour me another, and I'll tell you my thoughts on what should have been. And with one for the road, I'll give you a few hindsight observations on what would have been.

Coulda, shoulda, woulda.

And that was pretty much my life for about ten years. No magic … just that.

Rock Bottom

In January 1999, much to my surprise, I finally had that moment of being in the right place at the right time with the right person. The place was my apartment, the time was one hungover morning, and the person was me.

I groggily woke up from a blackout in a stupor. All I remember is that a friend had called me the night before and asked if I wanted to go out for a couple of beers. I said yes to him and said to myself, "It'll just be one or two." And now here I found myself in bed with no recollection of how I had gotten home. I called my friend on the premise of just seeing how he was and found out I'd almost gotten in a fight at the bar. I didn't remember that.

I was finally scared ... of me and my addictions. I decided I had to do something. I had to get clean and sober. Little did I know that I had taken the first step toward not only living without drink and drugs but also living—period. For me, the party had to end.

It just so happened that I had a therapy session that afternoon, and the first words out of my mouth when I sat down on my therapist's couch were "I need help. I have a problem." He had been waiting for me to say those words, because if he had said them to me, they wouldn't have had the same impact.

I decided to go into an outpatient rehab in Manhattan and went to an Alcoholics Anonymous (AA) meeting that afternoon. I've not had a drink since then, one day at a time.

The meeting I went to was held in a church at noon, and it was full of businesspeople, theater people, a sampling of just about every demographic. That meeting became my home group, and I went there every Monday through Friday. I went to other meetings over the weekend.

I embraced AA, and the recovering members of those meetings

embraced me. The step I took in admitting I had a problem led me to the twelve steps that helped me stay sober.

So, I'd go to rehab in the morning, to my noontime meeting, and then to work. And when work was over, I went straight home. What a difference a day makes. For me, that day was January 25, 1999.

Ninety Days

With the help of the twelve steps and a group of loving, caring recovering alcoholics who took me in, I stayed clean and sober one day at a time. Working those twelve steps with a group of loving, caring recovering alcoholics made my journey toward recovery a joyful one.

Reaching ninety days of sobriety is a big moment in New York AA groups. On that anniversary, the newcomer shares a bit of his or her story in front of the group. I was so accustomed to giving my testimony during my Christian days; this was quite similar. A sober testimony. I mention my Christian days because during my brief celebratory talk to the group, I said that I had found more unconditional love and acceptance in AA than I had in any church or Christian group I had encountered. And, unfortunately for the state of the church, I truly meant it.

I was aware that most of these new recovering people in my life talked a great deal of a Higher Power, bringing back into my world, after a long absence, the concept of God. Only this God they talked about wasn't the one I had walked away from years ago. This God had no definitive description, other than loving those who had hit the bottom in their lives. Everyone's definition of God didn't have to be the same. That was freedom I never thought possible. All I could say, at the beginning of my sobriety, was that this Higher Power was greater than myself. Once I realized that, my life began to change. I began to change. As I'd hear in the meetings, "Nothing changes if nothing changes."

As one day at a time went by, the days became weeks, the weeks turned into months, and those months quickly became two years. I was staying sober. And along with sobriety came clarity—about myself, about my life. And out of clarity grew self-respect, and the belief that life was now something to embrace, not hide from. And I found I could embrace the concept of a Higher Power.

For too long, I had lived my life as if it were something to be endured, not explored. I was unearthing the sense of hope that fear had long covered. The fear of failure and of not getting it right, and of being a disappointment to God. I had allowed discouragement to become despair. With newfound hope, I rediscovered the goals that I had long ignored and the dreams that had been dashed by disappointments.

For once, I felt entitled to fulfillment, to happiness, to living life "beyond my wildest dreams." I simply started to want more for my life. It seemed daring to want to be happy.

I allowed myself to question choices I had made. Those life choices came from decisions that I had let circumstances and situations make for me.

One of those biggest choices had been my life's work. As for my career, I had long ago stopped looking for what I wanted, settling for what I thought I needed, or should need. Perhaps it was time to ask myself what I truly wanted—what I wanted to be doing. Time to look at whatever gifts or talents I might have; time to believe it was okay to want to use them.

The habits of living life one way are not that easily broken. I wasn't yet ready, or prepared, to leap into the new and unknown. But I entered our new century believing change was possible.

Rumor Has It

During the month of January 2001, rumors began to spread throughout the staff at work that our law firm was going to either close shop or merge with a larger firm. After weeks of speculation and second-guessing on the staff's part, it was announced that, at the end of May, the firm would, indeed, merge with a big law firm downtown.

Because I was sober, I allowed myself to question what this merger might mean for me. It certainly seemed like an opportune time to again question just what I wanted to do with my life. I could stay with this job or explore new options. But even though I now had a chance to consider change, I was just as anxious as everyone else over whether I'd still have my job after the merger anyway.

A new rumor started that not everyone on staff would be going to the new firm. That rumor was quickly confirmed. As for our small word-processing department, there was me and the daytime word processor. Only one of us would go to the new firm.

I was flattered that our attorneys wanted me to work in the word-processing center of the new firm. I would have a different schedule from the one I had had for the past thirteen years. I would now work with three other word processors on a regular daytime shift of 8:30 in the morning to 4:30 in the afternoon. I asked if I could take a couple of days to think about it.

Now that my fears were eased, and I knew I still had a job, I was at the proverbial fork in the road of decisions. I was confused and went back and forth in my mind about both roads. On the one hand, I could stick with a job that offered a steady paycheck. On the other hand, this might be an opportunity to go back to some of those dreams that I had filed under "I can't" or "It wouldn't work." It was a decision that could change the direction of my life.

I talked with friends, my fellow AA members. I even resorted to praying to my Higher Power about it.

I felt like I stood on the edge of a cliff, looking out at the expanse of possibilities before me. Could I take what would have to be a leap of faith, and turn down the job and just jump out into the unknown? That would be a huge leap.

At the end of May, the firm packed up, closed its doors, and, on June 1, 2001, merged with the other firm and moved to its offices downtown—across from the World Trade Center.

And I went with it.

Glorious Summer

Our offices were at 195 Broadway, between Fulton Street to the north and Dey Street to the south. The building stood directly behind the Millennium Hotel, which was on Church Street and faced the World Trade Center. To get there, all you had to do was go out one of the revolving doors of our lobby onto Dey Street and walk a few yards forward, and you'd be on Church Street, which is where I was during most of 9/11.

It only took a few days of working at our new offices for me to cherish working by the World Trade Center. I had certainly gone there before in all my years of living in New York, usually when friends or family visited and I took on the role of tour guide. All they were interested in was going up to the observation deck. I assumed that was the only main attraction of the Twin Towers. What I was unaware of was that those Twin Towers and the other World Trade Center buildings that surrounded them and the mall beneath them were like a city within the city.

I immediately loved working a day shift. Since I had become sober, getting up early was no longer the problem it once was. I made it a point to get up and ready for work so I would get downtown early. I soon developed a daily routine.

I'd leave my apartment and head to Good and Plenty, a small café, where I'd get my first cup of coffee for the morning and a bagel or pastry. Since it was summer, I'd sit at one of the outdoor tables and eat what amounted to my breakfast.

I lived in Midtown Manhattan, in the neighborhood known as Hell's Kitchen. I'd go to the subway and take a train down to the stop before the World Trade Center. Then I'd come up onto the street, out of the subway, by 8:00 a.m. and start walking the few blocks toward the World Trade Center.

The streets were always dotted with the familiar sight of shiny aluminum carts, with just enough space for a person to stand inside and serve coffee, bagels, and assorted pastries. My first morning, I stopped at one, and I went to the same cart on the same corner across from Building Number 5 every morning, including September 11.

I didn't know his name, and he didn't know mine, but the man in that cart became my "coffee man." Within my first week, he had memorized how I liked my coffee, which I think he tried to do for all his regular customers. Every day, he greeted me with a "Good morning, my friend" and had my large coffee (half regular, half decaf with skim milk, Sweet'N Low on the side) ready for me by the time I got my dollar out. If I happened to miss stopping by any given morning, he'd ask me where I had been the next time he saw me. That's a New Yorker for you!

I'd then stop at the same newsstand and get that morning's newspaper on my way to the World Trade Center plaza. I'd go sit on one of the stone-slab benches around the perimeter of the fountain at the World Trade Center, reading the newspaper while drinking my coffee. I would also watch the people passing me on their way to work. And the tourists who decided to make the Twin Towers first on their day's itinerary.

Often, during that morning ritual of mine, I felt comforted that my life was good. When the weather was favorable, the sky a bright blue, and the summer breeze light and warm, in those quiet minutes alone, it seemed that all was right with the world, just as it did that morning in September.

If the weather was bad, there was the massive shopping mall below those looming towers—a perfect refuge and an ideal place to pass extra time. It had an array of stores and shops to look through and several places to get something to eat. I also spent many a lunch hour in the bookstore in Building Number 5 flipping through a magazine, looking for that next good book to read, or listening to CDs in the music section.

But, my favorite thing to do at lunchtime, if the weather permitted, was to sit in that expansive plaza area watched over by not only the towers but also the other buildings of the World Trade Center. It was summer, and summer at the World Trade Center was glorious.

At lunchtime, the plaza would fill up with people and activity, vendors selling hot dogs or ice cream or pretzels; people who were part of the community of workers would eat their lunches (brought from home or bought from there); the men would have their suit jackets off, their ties loosened, and their top shirt buttons undone; the women, in their business attire, would sit with their shoes kicked off. People would be getting a head start on their tans, sitting within and around the plaza area, heads tilted back, facing the sun, getting those few important minutes of sun time.

There were the tourists, identifiable by the inevitable cameras around their necks or in their hands. Though they were easy targets to poke fun at, they're the ones who reminded me of the magic of this city, seeing in their expressions and hearing in their exclamations the astonishment of what they were experiencing all around them.

In the center of the plaza, there was the fountain, balancing a sphere sculpted by the German sculptor Fritz Koenig atop it. It was a stylized globe made of different-color metals. It sat right in the middle of the fountain, which was circled by one continuous bench. I often sat there, my own face up to the sun, listening to the soft sound of the water spilling over into the fountain's bottom. If I closed my eyes, I could pretend I was near an ocean shore—very relaxing.

During the summer months, there were free noontime concerts in the plaza. Rows of folding chairs faced a temporary stage of steel and metal. Each day, a specific style of music was performed live: jazz, country, bebop, doo-wop, or my favorite—"golden oldies." Here I'd be, in the middle of New York, in the middle of my workday, listening to Peter Noone of Herman's Hermits one day, Mark Lindsay of Paul Revere and the Raiders another. On those golden oldies days, people would get up out of their folding chairs and dance in front of the stage or right where they were—an elderly couple here, two female coworkers laughing while dancing over there, the maintenance man, the businessman, the young secretary, everyone forgetting they would soon head back to work, and, oh yes, the tourists smiling for the picture being taken of them dancing away.

Perhaps I idealize it, now that it's gone, but I don't think so. It was an oasis for the worker on a tedious workday, a fascination for the visitor seeing the sights, a small world of its own that held some of the elements that make New York so dynamic, so interesting, and oh so alive.

It had a heart all its own.

That Beautifully Blue Sky

There was something special about that eleventh day of September 2001. Perhaps it had something to do with how beautiful a day it was, the sky being the most stunning shade of azure blue I'd ever seen. It was a color that defied description. That is the one thing many people throughout the country mention when they talk about 9/11—what a beautiful day it was.

I myself was doing what I usually did each workday morning before I had to go into my office building. I was sitting on one of the stone-slab benches in the plaza area of the World Trade Center between the Twin Towers. My paper cup of coffee sat beside me, and I held my newspaper in my hands. There was something about that day specifically. And that something seemed to permeate the air around me and the motions of the people I watched heading to their jobs or wherever else they might have been going.

I was at a good place personally in my life, and because of that sky, the air, and the atmosphere created all around me, I truly felt that my life was good. I felt revitalized.

As 8:30 approached, I folded up the newspaper, crumbled up the paper coffee cup, throwing it away, and headed toward one of the revolving side doors on Dey Street. I took one of the elevators up to the twenty-third floor and headed to the word-processing center, where my desk was.

At 8:30, I picked up my first work assignment and turned on my computer and started typing. In sixteen minutes, my life, our country, and the world would never be the same again.

8:46 a.m.

The shudder of our building and the loud, thunderous booming sound happened simultaneously. We were experiencing either an earthquake or the loudest thunder I had ever heard. But loud enough to make a building shake?

The movement of our building and the deafening sound stopped, it seemed, in a moment's time. My coworkers and I looked at one another. I don't know for certain, but I think I was the first to say, "What was that?" Others in the office threw out rapid guesses for us to consider. Was it thundering? Did something explode? Was it a bomb? Did a construction crane fall to the street?

During this impromptu guessing game, our phone rang. Someone answered it. She listened briefly, then said it was our manager who had not yet left for work, screaming into the phone something about a plane and the World Trade Center and for us to get out of the building. Those words only added to the puzzlement of what had just happened.

I don't remember how long it took before someone ran into the word-processing center where we worked and told us that a plane had hit one of the World Trade Center towers. It seemed like seconds but was probably at least a few minutes.

I forget who it was who ran into our center, but she told us that a secretary, who had just come to work, was hysterical, saying that a plane had hit one of the towers and that it was like a war zone out there. The person telling us this could have been speaking in another language because what she had just told us was so beyond reason. In trying to make sense of what I had just heard, I imagined that it must be a very small private plane. Perhaps the person piloting it had had a heart attack or miscalculated his or her navigation. That was the only sensible reality I could comprehend at that time. I brushed aside the comment of it being like a war zone outside the confines and comfort of our office.

After creating a more reasonable scenario in my head, I had an instinct to go downstairs and see for myself—more out of curiosity than out of alarm. So, I went to the elevator bank, along with a few other people who I guess had the same idea. As we descended from the twenty-third floor, I convinced myself that a light plane had to have smashed into the tower. I imagined a small hole in the building, with the back end of the plane sticking out. The thought of anyone having died never entered my mind.

During those moments it took for the elevator car to get to the lobby, our conversation was tinged with nervousness but not fear.

Once we reached the lobby and the elevator doors opened, I took a quick right and walked through the same revolving side door I had entered to begin my workday. As I passed through that door and out onto Dey Street, three things went through my mind. One, the secretary was right; it did look like a war zone. Two, it also looked like a movie set for a disaster film. And three, it was like going through the door in *The Wizard of Oz*, walking out into a world that was unlike anything that I could ever have possibly imagined.

Looking back now, I know as the revolving door turned with me in it, I was about to leave the Artie that I was at that moment, and as I passed through that door and out onto Dey Street, I was about to have my life torn apart, leaving who I once was behind in that lobby.

Out onto the Street

The first thing I noticed, as my foot hit the sidewalk, was that I had stepped down ankle-deep into sheets of paper of all sorts and sizes. It was everywhere—the paper. It lined the sidewalk and filled the pavement all the way to Church Street.

It was like stepping into a snowstorm. Everything was white—as far as I could see—like a surreal blanket of freshly fallen snow. Sheets of paper were coming down from the sky above me. Whole sheets of paper and scraps of paper and bits of paper floating down from as far up as I could see. I had never seen so much paper.

As I began to walk the few steps to Church Street, I noticed other objects on the ground. Clusters of insulation and pieces of what looked like plasterboard. Twisted shapes of metal. Thinking back, I don't know if I was seeing shards of the plane or the North Tower. I think other things also lay among all that paper, which my mind refuses to let me remember.

In any event, my attention left the ground as, with those few steps toward Church Street, my head tilted upward, finally letting the North Tower become my focus. Oh my God! What should have been just a small hole with the back end of a little plane sticking out was a huge canyon blasted into the side of the tower. Smoke, the thickest and blackest I've ever seen, billowed from the gaping wound. Flames of the brightest oranges and reds shot out from the blackness.

I know that, in the back of my mind, the thought that people were dead had to be registering, but right then, I couldn't get past just staring at the destruction of the tower and thinking about how bad it looked.

My senses came into play. Aside from what my eyes were seeing, I became aware of the sound of sirens. They seemed to be coming from everywhere. I smelled the mixture of jet fuel and burning building materials, breathing in particles from all those smells. It's difficult to write this, but I also know that included among those particles going down into my lungs were those of burnt human remains.

The surrounding buildings were starting to evacuate, and the streets were filling up with people. Behind me, a crowd had already gathered, everyone doing as I was, staring at the burning, smoking North Tower in absolute shock. I don't believe any of us had the mental capabilities at that point to register how catastrophic it was.

From the floors above, where the plane had created that gaping canyon, I could see people who must have broken through the glass of the windows because some were leaning out, waving articles of clothing, their way of silently screaming, "We're trapped up here! Help us, please!" I imagine the flames and smoke below them were making their way up, filling their offices. We could see the people in the most danger were standing on the ledges of the broken-out windows, trying to get away from the smoke and fire. In a moment that seemed to freeze in time, I witnessed the first person plunging down the length of the North Tower. All I remember is a woman behind me screaming as I also began to scream.

I screamed the word "No!"

Onto the Battlefield

I continued screaming, "No! No! No!" as I stood in the street watching one person after another plunging down the length of the North Tower.

I knew they were jumping to avoid the thick black smoke and the flames that surrounded them, but I wanted to stop them—to stop this awful reality. I wanted each "No!" that I screamed to stop the people from hitting the ground. I wanted my shouts to push them back up to where they had jumped from.

The fight-or-flight response kicked in, and I chose to fight. I felt compelled to try to help them, and without a moment's thought or hesitation, I just started running toward the North Tower. I ran past a photographer quickly snapping pictures. I ran past the stone benches I used to sit on. I ran through that blizzard of falling paper, running up the steps leading to the plaza.

Once up the steps, I was forced to stop at the southeast corner of Building Number 5, under the protection of an overhang. The North Tower was right across from me, the distance of only half a block, looming upward. The only thing separating me from the tower was a section of the plaza, where huge pieces of twisted metal shapes were crashing onto the concrete, each impact booming thunderously. Large shards of glass from blown-out windows fell steadily, sounding like a hard hailstorm as piece after piece hit the ground, shattering.

I wanted to run across the plaza toward the tower, but there was all that debris falling, along with more people. I know that my mind has blocked some of the images I had to have seen as I witnessed bodies hitting the ground. At one point, it looked like a person had fallen onto a pile of clothes, but I know it was really a pile of bodies.

Frantically looking around, I saw that the overhang I stood under went along the length of Building Number 5, and I thought maybe I could run around to the tower, protected by the overhang, and get closer to the people on the ground. All rationale escaped my mind at that point because no one could have survived falling from such heights. But I thought maybe there was a chance someone was miraculously still living and I could pull him or her to safety. Or, if someone was gasping a few last breaths, I could hold his or her hand until help came or until that last breath. Something inside me ached, not wanting anyone to die alone. But reality came crashing through my wall of well-meaning intentions, and I knew there was nothing I could do without putting my own life in jeopardy. For the first time in my life, I knew what it was like to feel totally helpless. It is a gut-wrenching feeling. And I was faced with the challenge of whether I was willing to risk my own life.

Before I could meet that challenge, another man ran up and stood beside me. My attention was taken away from him because something caught my eye. I looked up and to my left and saw a man in a dark business suit falling. But this time, much closer to me, and with much greater detail. I couldn't take my eyes off him, and as he neared the ground, I clearly saw how frantically his arms and legs moved, as if he was desperately trying to slow himself down. As I was about to see him hit the ground, his descent took him behind the stage where I had watched those noontime concerts.

I turned to the man who had joined me and asked, "What do we do?" He didn't have an answer, and he and I stood and stared as one body after another fell. Again, I believe the saving grace of blocked memories kicked in, though part of me wants to remember everything.

The bodies and debris kept falling, and then shouts from two guards drew our attention to a side entrance of Building Number 5, where they were holding the door open and screaming for me and the man beside me to get in. One last quick look at the intensity of the wreckage and people falling into the plaza convinced us we had no choice. If we wanted to live, we had to run toward the two guards, not toward the North Tower. Fortunately for us, we had that overhang over us that went along the side of Building Number 5, so we ran under it and through the door the guards held open for us. We were pulled into a crowd of people evacuating the building, like cattle in a stampede. We went out a front entrance right onto Church Street, next to my favorite bookstore.

I pushed through the crowded streets and sidewalks and found myself standing in front of the Century 21 store near the South Tower. I stood, along with so many others, as we continued to watch people falling to their deaths. For me, it was not out of morbid curiosity. I don't think that was anyone's reason for doing that. I think we, as the witnesses of so many deaths, watched because the falling people deserved to not be alone. They weren't alone even though we were far from them in the safety of the street.

Those trapped on the top floors above that black canyon blasted into the tower knew they were going to die. Their last decision in life was to choose how they would die, either by fire and smoke or by taking that leap from above. I consider those who were irreverently labeled "the jumpers" courageous individuals, and I have the utmost respect for them. I can't imagine what it would be like to have to face the decision of how your life will end. To me, they were heroically brave and deserved our dignity as witnesses to the choice they had made.

I only stood there for a few moments, however, before the others and I heard the incredibly loud sound of an airplane—the second plane as it approached the South Tower.

The Second Plane

Looking up and to my left, I saw the plane was so big, and so close to the tops of the buildings it passed. My first thought was that the air-traffic controllers had gotten mixed up and were misdirecting planes. At that moment, that made the most sense to me. So, I stared at the plane, believing it would pull up in time before getting to the tower.

The middle floors of the tower blew outward in a massive inferno of bright orange flames and dense clouds of black smoke upon impact. Time stood still for just a second, as if we all were suspended in disbelief. In the next beat, pandemonium broke out. Screaming, panic, mass confusion. I, along with all the others in the street, just started running, literally running for our lives. Twisted metal, glass, and other debris rained down on us. I ran toward Fulton Street, at one point thinking that I was going to run right out of my loafers. As I turned east onto Fulton, I slipped and fell to my hands and knees. People stepped on top of me, pushing me to the ground, and I thought that I would be trampled to death. But I got back on my feet and started running. I remember running and screaming out loud, "God save us all!"

I looked behind my left shoulder and saw an African American woman and a Caucasian businessman running together. She tripped and began falling to the street, but the man grabbed her arm and pulled her up. Even during pure horror, I was touched by the act of goodness.

I looked to my right and saw a man scrambling to get under a van. He was dressed in a suit and lay on his back, desperately trying to slither beneath the vehicle for protection. I remember glancing at his face, and our eyes locked for one brief second, a look of sheer terror on his face.

Up ahead of me, a man lay on his stomach in the middle of Fulton Street. He was a heavyset man in a suit. Everyone was running right by him. I ran past him, but for whatever reason, I stopped and ran back to him. I dropped to my knees at his side. It was then I noticed all the blood and where it was coming from. His skull had been split open, and the top part of his brain was protruding through the split. Blood gushed out of the wound. Amazingly, he was breathing, although unconscious. I saw lying near his head a putty knife—a regular-looking putty knife that had an almost-even line of blood on its blade. I thought, *Oh my God, is this what hit him?* I remember putting it back down as another man came running over, dropping down on his knees beside me to my right. Someone handed a denim jacket to me, saying, "Take this." I took it, and the other man and I applied it over the opening in the man's skull. The other man put his hand on top of mine, and we held the jacket there with all the pressure we could summon, trying desperately to slow down the flow of blood.

Now that the falling debris had lessened, people were stopping, and others ran over to us. An ambulance was on Church Street. We all started screaming for it. "Over here! Over here!"

As the ambulance began to make its way toward us, through the debris in the street, someone who said he or she knew first aid suggested we turn the man over onto his back. Four of us did so, carefully. His teeth were covered with blood and dirt or soot or something, and I used my fingers to clean out his mouth. I noticed his watch lying there beside him, it having come off. I picked it up and put it in his left pants pocket.

His employee work tag hung around his neck. I didn't really look at it. I wish now that I had. I wish that I had looked at his name and where he worked and memorized them. I doubt he survived such a severe wound, and I would want to find his family and tell them that he wasn't alone—that he had people with him. That is my biggest regret of that day, along with the regret of not finding a way to get to the North Tower. I'm prone to think "if only" often.

The ambulance reached us, and a flat board was brought over. The unconscious man was so big it took at least six of us to gingerly get him onto it. He was belted to the board, and we lifted him and carried him to the back of the ambulance. I was at the front of the board, to the right of his head. I remember rubbing his arm back and forth and whispering continually into his ear, "You'll be okay. You'll be okay."

As the ambulance began maneuvering up Fulton Street, I followed it up to Broadway. Then I looked at my hands and saw that they were covered with the man's blood. There, I saw another ambulance on Broadway already treating some of those with minor injuries. I went up to one of the EMS workers and just showed her my hands. At first, she thought the blood was coming from me, but I told her, "No ... it's someone else's." She had me sit down on the curb and said she would come right over to wash my hands.

As I sat on the curb, a man in a suit looked down at me and asked if I was okay. Another random act of goodness, a stranger concerned about another stranger. I was touched by that brief exchange.

The EMS worker soon returned. She knelt in front of me and began cleaning my hands with liquid from a bottle. I looked her in the eyes and asked, "What's going on?" I remember her looking me in the eyes and saying, "I don't know, but this is awful."

She helped me up from the curb and went to attend to others. I was in front of my office building now, and I saw one of my coworkers. I went up to her, and we hugged. She later told me I was shaking like a leaf.

There were more screams, and our attention was drawn to the South Tower, where, just like at the North Tower, brave individuals were plunging down from the top floors of the tower, above the black canyon that had been blasted into it. So, we watched and screamed each time we witnessed each person falling. They were not alone in their deaths—none of them. We were all there to bear witness.

Suddenly, I realized that as I watched this horror unfold, my parents were seeing it as well on TV. I had left my cell phone at my desk. The lines at the pay phones were already very long, so I started going up to people, asking, "Can I use your cell phone?"—but none of their phones were working. I started walking north, asking anyone with a cell phone I encountered if his or her phone was working. Some were, some weren't, but no one would let me make my call.

Finally, a few blocks north, I darted into a coffee shop that was empty except for a few of its workers. There was a man behind the counter, and I simply shouted, "Can I use your phone?" In a daze, he motioned toward the back, where I ran to. There was a Hispanic girl on the phone, crying and speaking in Spanish. As soon as she hung up, I picked up the receiver, but my mind drew a blank, and I couldn't remember my parents' phone number.

I could only remember one number, and it was that of a friend who worked uptown. Amazingly, I got through to him and simply yelled into the phone, "Billy, it's Artie. Call my parents. I can't remember their number.

Van Why. In Millersville, or Lancaster. Pennsylvania. Tell them I'm okay. Okay?" I hung up.

I walked out of the coffee shop, which was about three blocks north of the towers, onto a street filled with people. Simultaneously, yet another massive explosive sound rang out as the street buckled beneath us. We seemed to stop where we were, all of us looking at one another. We had no idea that it was the South Tower collapsing. Suddenly, coming toward us from the south was a huge wall of a dust cloud, immense in size. In frenzied confusion, everyone looked at one another, not knowing what to do. Some started screaming. Panicking, we all just started running north, away from the approaching, nebulous wall of debris, dust, and smoke rapidly moving toward us. My thoughts were *What in God's name is happening?* and *What is that cloud, and what is in it?*

People continued to scream; others cried hysterically. I just kept running. I had never run so fast in my life. I ran until I couldn't run anymore. I had to stop, gasping for breath. I looked behind me and saw that I had outrun the dust cloud. The dust was now settling on the street and the buildings and sidewalks and the cars parked next to them. Just as it had been with all that paper, there was now nothing but dull, gray dust everywhere. I was breathing it in.

I debated whether I should go back down to the towers to help. But my fight-or-flight response caused me to take flight this time, and probably saved my life. If I had gone back down to the now-destroyed towers, I probably would have taken some action among the rubble that would have put me in danger. So, instead, I began the long walk home to Midtown Manhattan, along with everyone else, in absolute silence.

An Obvious Stillness

There was an obvious stillness in the air as the hordes of us walked, dazed and shocked, uptown. Thousands of us. Strangers. A mass of silent humanity walking together.

I remember seeing a woman's high-heel shoe lying in the street and wondering if she was still walking with just one shoe on.

Getting closer to Midtown, I noticed people on the street corners gathered around radios. I began hearing whispers of "the Pentagon" and "Pennsylvania." I knew then that those planes' hitting the towers was no accident. It was then that I realized something terrible was happening.

Halfway home, at Fifth Avenue, I reached the office of my friend Billy (whom I had called) and went up to it in the elevator. Some of his coworkers grabbed and hugged me, as did Billy. I really couldn't speak at that point except to ask where the restroom was. I went in and washed the dust and dirt off my face. My knees were throbbing, so I pulled up my pant legs. Both knees were bleeding from when I fell in the street.

After I finished in the restroom, Billy and I went to the elevator to go to the street and meet up with his boyfriend. The three of us continued the slow walk back to Midtown (where we all lived). We, like almost everyone else, instinctively started veering west as we neared Midtown, veering away from the Empire State Building.

It was a little after noon when I finally arrived at my apartment on West Forty-Third Street. I saw that my answering machine was blinking with I don't remember how many messages. I sat down on my bed and tried to think of what to do next. At some point, I looked down and saw that I had put on a pair of shorts. I don't remember doing that. I stared at my scraped knees, still bleeding. I ignored them, trying to think of what to do next. Every circuit in my brain was on overload; anxiety, images, and thoughts ran rampant. I needed to get out of my apartment. But then what?

The Meeting and the Vigil

As if thrown a life preserver, I remembered the noontime twelve-step meeting in my neighborhood that I had gone to every weekday before my firm moved downtown. That was where I would go. I assumed it wouldn't be as packed as usual, but I knew at least some people would be there. For many, it would be a place of solace. So, leaving my apartment building, I began walking to the church in Times Square where the meeting was held each day. I remember constantly looking up at the sky as I walked the streets, which had no moving cars and few people.

When I walked in, the meeting was at its midpoint. The turnout was much smaller than usual, as I had thought it would be, and the mood much more somber. I heard a woman say, just as I walked in, "I'm worried about the people I know who work down there." She saw me enter and said, "But one of them just walked in." All eyes were on me as I took a seat. I raised my hand to speak and began sobbing, trying to find the words to describe, for the first time, what I had witnessed.

There was a man I didn't know sitting to my left. I remember he was wearing a white chef's jacket. He brought his chair closer to me and put his arm around me. When I could speak no longer, he kept his arm around me for the remainder of the meeting. As soon as it ended, others came over to me, hugging me, holding me. In a way, I felt safely at home.

Some of the men walked me home, one stopping at a drugstore to get something I hadn't thought of. He got bandages for my knees.

We got to Good and Plenty, the café across from my apartment building, and we sat around one of the outdoor tables. Someone handed me his or her cell phone, asking if I wanted to call my parents. This time, I remembered their number and dialed it. My mom answered. All I remember saying, in what probably sounded like a desensitized tone, was that I was okay but couldn't really talk (talking about it at the meeting had drained me) and that we would talk later.

Once I left the café and that group of men, I went back to my apartment. I really can't remember what I did then. I do know I called the therapist I was seeing at the time and asked if he could see me the next day. He found time for me in the morning. After that, most of the rest of that day is lost to me. I can't remember if I called any of my friends. I don't even know if I had anything to eat.

That evening, I instinctively headed to one of the firehouses in my neighborhood. I knew there would be people there. And, at that time, I needed to be with people, especially other New Yorkers. As I had surmised, there were people standing in front of the firehouse. A memorial had already been put together with pictures of the men from that company who had presumably lost their lives. There were flowers and lit candles.

It wasn't a huge group, so I easily made my way to the front to be directly in front of the makeshift memorial. I got down on my knees and looked at the photos of the men who had not come back with their company. Some of the candles had blown out. There was a box of matches on the sidewalk. I picked up the box and began relighting the candles that had lost their flames.

Behind me, someone started singing a patriotic song (I can't remember which it was), and one by one, we all joined in the singing until it sounded, to me, like a choir of angels. Singing that song as a group was a display of the resolve New Yorkers would display in the weeks and months that followed. We would be united.

I continued to sit there, and while doing so, a microphone was put in front of my face, held by a television reporter from who knows where. He asked me some question about how I was feeling at that moment. I have no idea what answer I gave him. I was still in shock and unable to think. But he wasn't rude about it. He had asked if it was okay to ask me the question. I believed he was a foreign correspondent by his accent, and thinking that, I realized at that moment that this was a global event that went way past just the isle of Manhattan. What had happened that morning didn't just affect New Yorkers. It was a far-reaching act of terrorism affecting the world.

I left the vigil and walked home. I finally talked to my parents around midnight, although I mostly just cried. I hadn't realized till talking to them just how close I had come to being among those who lost their lives that day. I should have felt lucky to be alive, but at that moment I didn't.

The Next Morning

The morning after 9/11 was the first time I wrote down my story of witnessing and surviving the previous day's terrorist attack. I woke up the morning of September 12 after an erratic attempt to sleep during the night. I slept with my nightstand light on, which I continued to do for about a year. I do that some nights even now, a remaining symptom of post-traumatic stress disorder.

That morning, I listened to all the voicemails that people had left me and read all the emails that had been sent, all from family and friends, everyone wanting to know if I was safe. If I was alive.

I didn't have the energy to return every call or respond to every email, so I sat at my computer, ready to send a mass email to everyone just to let them know I was okay. But when my fingers touched the keyboard, I started typing rapidly, in a stream of consciousness, writing down in words for the first time the events of the morning before.

I was honest and precise, holding back nothing.

I wrote of the sound of the massive explosion of the first plane hitting the North Tower.

I depicted walking out into the war zone that the streets encompassing the World Trade Center had become.

I described the sounds, the smells, the sights.

Falling debris, falling people.

The screams, the blood.

The moments I thought my death was imminent.

When I finished typing, I hit the Send button and the email went out. It seemed in minutes I started receiving responses. In each email, everyone thanked me for describing 9/11 and what I witnessed and went through. From my perspective, my experience provided for them an insight into the sheer horror that words in newspapers or images on television could never truly convey to them.

Those I had sent my email to forwarded it to people they knew, and I began receiving emails from around the country, each of them with similar words thanking me for sharing my experience. I had yet to realize just how powerful our stories can be.

It was early when I sent out that initial email, about seven in the morning. After that, I had to get out of my apartment, to be with other people. I walked out onto a street where there was no commotion. No cars on the street. No horns blaring. Only the occasional wail of a siren haunted the quiet. I remember the weather being, as it was the day before, beautiful.

I followed my daily routine and went to Good and Plenty across the street to get a cup of coffee. It was familiar, and I needed familiarity at that point. Crossing the street, I didn't know if it would be open, but it was. The owner, a woman, was standing in the middle of the café with what would become common among us all: a look of aftershock. I thanked her for being open, and she replied that she felt she "had to do something." She unnecessarily apologized because there would be no morning delivery of fresh-baked goods. She took what pastries and bagels she had left from the previous day and, along with large thermal urns of coffee, set up a table just outside, near the small tables. She didn't charge for any of it that morning. What she had she offered for free, to anyone who came by hoping to find the place open.

I sat at one of the tables, drinking my coffee. Other people, some of them recognizable regulars, began coming by, all people from the neighborhood. Each of them remarked how glad they were the place was open. I assume they, like me, needed to get away from the confines of their apartments. Most took a seat at one of the tables. We started speaking with one another, started to put words to our thoughts. I was reminded of family wakes I had gone to as a child, where, after the funeral, family members would gather together for food and comfort and support. That's what we all were doing that morning. Neighbors, some of us complete strangers to one another, were coming together. We, and the city, had begun to mourn.

Mornings

Mornings were the hardest for me. For everyone in New York, probably. I would have that one brief second when, waking up, my mind was still a bit unfocused. That brief second of disconnection from the real world. In an instant, though, reality pushed its way to the forefront. The images and sounds of that awful morning flooded back into my thoughts.

I couldn't turn the television on that week. I had tried to watch a bit of the coverage the previous evening, but I had to turn it off. I couldn't watch one more replay of the towers being struck, of people falling, of buildings collapsing. My personal experience was enough. I didn't need other people's images. I didn't turn my television on for weeks and weeks, until the nonstop coverage had ceased. And even then, the moment a newsbreak or story came on about the aftermath of the terrorist attack, I turned off the set.

I couldn't look at or read a newspaper. I didn't need to be reminded in print of what had taken place. I couldn't look at front pages, couldn't read headlines. The first time I did buy a paper after the eleventh, I turned a page at one point only to see a picture of a man, in midair, stopped by the camera as he fell from the North Tower.

On the day after 9/11, after I had gone from Good and Plenty back to my apartment, I called my parents. I couldn't really speak. All I could do was cry.

As the days passed, I tried not to isolate myself. I met with friends each day. I went to my therapist's office as often as I could and attended that noontime meeting each day. In the office of my therapist and the comfort of the meetings, I could talk, cry, and express anger, grief, confusion, and fear.

I was grateful I wasn't drinking, because if I had been, I would have numbed with alcohol every feeling I had. Every emotion I experienced. I would have felt nothing, that's true, but I also would have been oblivious to what was happening. I would have shut down. As extreme and as painful as each day was following that awful morning, I faced it. I felt it. I'm so glad

I did. One thing I instinctively knew: I had to keep talking about what I had seen and what I was feeling. I continued to call my parents early each morning during the first few days and just cry.

I continued to sleep with a light on each night and began having anxiety attacks (another symptom of my PTSD). I went to my regular doctor, hoping medication might help me with these attacks. While in the examination room, I told him my story of 9/11 and I brought up the horribly injured man with the split skull. I asked my doctor if he thought the man could have survived such a severe wound. My doctor hesitated, but softly said, "No." I broke down and sobbed. But crying had become commonplace.

During the following days, I must have written three or four more emails, sharing what it was like to be in the city during the weeks after 9/11. And the responses of gratefulness continued coming back to me. And everyone encouraged me to continue writing. Which I did.

The Handbills

One of the hardest things in those first weeks was passing the countless handbills that went up all over the city—each with a different face and the bold word MISSING across the top. As the days went on and the number of those handbills grew, looking at that word became gut-wrenching, knowing that these strangers on the handbills, these people loved and worried about, were not merely missing. But, to use any word other than MISSING would be to admit that hope was fading. And, as each day passed into another, the city waited, praying for a miracle recovery of even one lone survivor.

Each handbill had a photocopied picture of the missing loved one. The photos ran the gamut of life itself. There were photos of brides smiling, someone ready to blow out candles on a cake, a father or mother with his or her children. Seeing glimpses into the personal moments of all these missing people was heartrending.

And as the weeks wore on, the handbills seemed to stick to the billboards and buildings and utility poles where they were pasted with a desperate determination to remain there despite the slight tears and rips caused by the wind, the print fading in the sun, and the word MISSING running from the rain onto the faces of those strangers.

The faces of the missing became the faces of victims. So many, many faces. I found myself wondering if I had passed any of them that morning on my way to work. Had I looked into the eyes of one of those faces and exchanged a glance or a smile? Did any of those faces belong to the people I saw falling to their deaths? I avoided the areas of the city where I knew there were a lot of handbills. It hurt too much, trying to take in the fact that so many people were gone, that so many had died.

Joe and Judd

On the Friday after the eleventh, two eight-by-ten photocopied pictures of two young men from my apartment building were taped to the glass door leading into our lobby. They had been roommates, friends since middle school. They had worked in the South Tower, for the same company, on the same floor. A makeshift memorial was already set up in our lobby: a table with a candle, a vase of flowers, and two bottles of beer.

The two young men had lived in an apartment on the first floor, along with two other friends. I didn't know any of their names. I referred to them as the *frat boys*, because they always threw parties and they looked as if they were just out of college. We would pass one another some mornings in our lobby on our way to work. I had no idea they worked at the World Trade Center.

One of the roommates was taping pictures of his friends to the wall where the memorial table had been set up. I told him how sorry I was and finally learned his name was Bert. His friends were Joe and Judd. Bert told me that, after the first plane had hit, one of the guys, I believe it was Judd, had called his girlfriend and said he and Joe were okay, and they were leaving the South Tower. That was the last anyone had heard from them.

I can't bear to think of how many spouses, partners, parents, sisters and brothers, and friends received a call from a loved one who was in one of the towers that morning, their loved one saying he or she was okay and leaving the office, but never came home.

Our apartment building became a close-knit community in those following weeks. Each day, the memorial in our lobby expanded. Arrangements of flowers, with their sweet scents, filled the surrounding floor space. Candles of all shapes and sizes were scattered among the bouquets. Stepping into the lobby from the elevator, one could feel the noticeable rise in temperature from the heat of all those candles, which stayed lit throughout the days and nights. The wall of condolences behind the display filled up with cards and messages from other tenants and with candid photos of Joe and Judd.

As people on the block became aware that two young men from the neighborhood were among those gone, they would pass our building's glass front, stopping to look at the memorial in our lobby. People would sometimes come in and add their flowers to the others.

I was still getting up early each day, so each morning, I went down to the lobby and, in the predawn quiet, scraped away dried candle wax from the tiled floor and replaced or relit those candles whose flames had gone out. I went to the fruit and vegetable market on our corner and bought fresh flowers to replenish those that were beginning to wilt. I didn't know those two young friends, those two frat boys, Joe and Judd, but I mourned their passing. Grieving them was a way for me to express my grief for all the lives that had been taken that day, thinking particularly of all those young, young men and women who, as they went to work that morning of the eleventh, had their whole lives ahead of them.

Not Letting Them Win

With my mind still in turmoil after 9/11, I had forgotten that my thirtieth high school reunion was that Saturday, September 15. An email from a classmate asking me if I still planned on coming reminded me. Not having gone to any of my other reunions, I had planned on going to this one. When I read my classmate's email, my immediate reaction was "No, of course not. I can't go now." I was still steeped in an ocean of emotions, shock being one of them. I also felt that I couldn't leave New York so soon. Not while New Yorkers were still in the early stages of grieving and mourning. It would be like leaving my family.

But, the president and our mayor placed great emphasis on how important it was to keep up with our daily routines—that we should not live frozen with fear of another attack. That is what the terrorist wanted from us. America was challenged to not give in to that fear. That caused me to question if my immediate reaction of not going was for the right reasons.

I talked to quite a few people I trusted and respected (including my therapist) about this dilemma and asked if they thought my choosing to not go was a good decision. I received opinions from all angles, and everyone told me that it was ultimately my decision to make. And they were right. I couldn't leave something this important to someone to tell me what to do. I had to do what my heart told me. For that to happen, I needed to be still and listen. I found going to my twelve-step meetings extremely beneficial. There, I could freely share what direction my heart and spirit were leading me toward.

I didn't want to play the victim, which, in my mind, would mean the terrorist had done to me what he wanted and he had me living in fear. As a result, I decided I would go to the reunion.

I rented a car to drive to Gaithersburg, where the reunion was being held. I left the city somewhat early that Saturday morning. Since New York is near several major airports, there were planes in the air since restrictions on flying had been lifted. As I was driving, a large plane flew over me fairly low, obviously preparing for landing. I say *obviously* because it was descending at a steady pace. It brought to my mind, immediately, the memory of the second plane, and I started to cry behind the wheel of the car. I was still afraid. But I was more determined not to let that fear put an end to my plan. So, I kept on driving.

I drove to my sister Sue's house in Damascus, Maryland, and my parents had driven down from Lancaster, Pennsylvania. Everyone wanted to see me, perhaps to confirm I had indeed survived.

When I walked through the front door, my dad greeted me first, with a quick hug. I say it was quick because he was about to burst into tears. That's the only greeting I remember. Though I was in a happy, and safe, environment, I operated on autopilot, still somewhat in shock. But then I was unaware of how the symptoms of PTSD were beginning to manifest in me.

I don't remember much about the reunion that evening except the reception I received from my former classmates was much warmer and heartfelt than it might have been under normal circumstances.

We were sitting at round tables (about ten to a table), and I was at one close to the front of the room. To start things off, the reunion head asked that we all stand one at a time and say where we had come from to see who had traveled the farthest.

They started at the back tables. One by one, old friends and acquaintances rose and stated where they were now from. It surprised me how many still lived in, or near, our hometown.

When it came time for my table, I remember standing and saying, with great pride, that I was from the greatest city in the world, New York. The response was thunderous as the room burst into wild applause. I quickly sat down, my back to the rest of the room. I was later told I hadn't seen the standing ovation given not just to me but to the city of New York. I don't think I ever felt prouder to be a New Yorker.

A Luncheon

One week following the attack, the employees of the law firm I worked for were called to meet at a hotel in Midtown. It was for a luncheon. More than that, though, it would be a time to face one another since 9/11, each of us with our own story of that morning.

All our employees had been accounted for after 9/11, except for one— one of our lawyers. He was a volunteer fireman for the town he lived in, outside the city. He was last seen running toward the towers, after the first plane had struck, doing what came so naturally to him, trying to help. He was now one of the "missing" and eventually became one of the "victims."

As I arrived at the luncheon, I could see people looking for their coworkers, the person they sat beside each day, the ones they ate lunch with. Our hugs were genuine, but our emotions were kept in place. We had coffee; we mingled, and we made some very, very small talk.

I looked at the faces, the expressions, the forced animation. No one wanted to talk about what we had all experienced just a week ago. We feigned interest in other topics of conversation. Only our eyes held the thoughts we were really thinking, the thoughts that were too difficult to put into words.

I found myself leaning against a wall, isolating myself from the group. I stood there, my mind filling with images of 9/11, as I fought back tears.

Eventually, we were called into the banquet room. It was filled with round tables, set beautifully. A podium, a microphone, and a piano stood on the raised platform in the front. We began finding tables to sit at, idle chatter filling the background. We could no longer dance around the subject at hand. It was time to address why we were there, time to answer the simple question, "Now what?"

On my seat lay a sheet of paper with the words to "America the Beautiful" printed on it. Someone went to the piano, and we were asked to stand and sing. This would be the second patriotic song I had heard, or sung, since the attack. The emotion and significance of the words pierced my heart. I could no longer hold back tears. As I cried, one of our lawyers, someone I didn't really know, came up and held me, and continued to hold me until the song was over.

I forget the order of that afternoon, as I've forgotten many things that happened during the weeks following the attack. Of course, opening remarks were made. Our missing lawyer was mentioned and given a moment of silence. His brother was introduced. He spoke of his brother—not quite a eulogy, yet the words he used to describe his brother were all in past tense.

A husband-and-wife team of grief counselors spoke to us. The firm had brought them in to provide individual and group counseling. They spoke briefly on what we might expect to go through—trauma, mourning, grief. I heard from them, for the first time, the words "post-traumatic stress disorder." It would be months before I understood what those words meant.

As they continued talking to us, a secretary broke down, sobbing, and had to be helped out of the room.

The luncheon was over.

Back to Work

My law firm's office building hadn't been structurally damaged, but it would be weeks before we could go back down to it. Until then, we, like so many other displaced companies, set up temporary offices in a hotel on the East Side in Midtown. Most everyone was working there before the second week was over. I couldn't bring myself to go. I called and spoke with my supervisor. I was told to take all the time I needed. I did.

Two or three weeks later, when I started back to work, I found that I could walk to the temporary office from my apartment. It was then that I realized I had been avoiding riding the subway.

Each morning walking there, I would look at the tall buildings as I passed them. I would visualize a plane crashing into them. I would map out my plan if it should happen. I wouldn't run from it. This time, I would run toward it. In my mind, this time I would help save lives. Or comfort the dying. I would have no regrets this time.

At work, the events of the morning of September 11 played over and over in my head. I think my mind was still trying to comprehend what had taken place that day—the sights and sounds and smells, the stickiness of that stranger's blood on my hands, the taste of burning ashes in the air.

How arbitrary it all had been as to who had died, who had lived. There were the incredible stories of people who had walked from the rubble, the stories of people who should have been there that morning but weren't, the stories of people who shouldn't have been down there but were.

I don't believe I witnessed the wrath of anyone's God that morning. What I did witness when I looked up at those burning towers was the ultimate evil that man is capable of. The evidence of just how deep hatred could run, how far it could go.

But I had also been a witness to something else that day—down on the ground. I witnessed the ultimate goodness of man, the evidence of how strong courage could be, to what lengths it would go.

I believe God or some Higher Power was in the hands of everyone who reached out to help someone else, and in the arms of people on the streets as they embraced one another, and in the tears of strangers who cried together, and in all the lives that were given in the line of duty, in the acts of heroism. And in the hearts of the people across the country who, as they watched the horror from afar, felt compassion.

The Grief Counselors

The husband-and-wife grief-counseling team that had been introduced to us employees at the luncheon began setting up group sessions in one of the hotel rooms, and, at the firm's urging, we were encouraged to take advantage of them.

I was more than willing to take part, having learned from my own personal therapy that it was important to continue to talk about what we were feeling and going through. I signed up for a specific time and was surprised to see the room full of about twenty people: some lawyers, secretaries, and other administrative staff.

The husband and wife encouraged us to talk openly and freely, assuring us this was a safe room to do just that. Only I and one of the lawyers spoke with emotion, both of us crying as we shared what we had witnessed on 9/11. I noticed that the remaining lawyers were very stiff, and if they said anything, they spoke as if they were in a courtroom. Most of them said they were doing okay and not being bothered by any of the PTSD symptoms that the counselors reemphasized.

I can't remember anyone else opening up as I and that lawyer did. It was a lesson in how people handle trauma and tragedy differently.

My Apartment

A few weeks later, I looked around my studio apartment and saw that it looked like a disaster area. By then, I had started buying newspapers, and I had strewn all the issues about the floor, as well as plastic Coke bottles. Empty coffee cups from the deli remained on whatever surface space had been near me when I finished drinking them. The brown bags they had been put into lay crumpled on the floor, as did discarded clothes. Dishes rose in a pile in the sink; trash cans overflowed.

There had been a subconscious design to this disarray. I had created a personal sanctum, a place that held near me the devastating effect of the morning of 9/11, a place where the elements of that horrific morning were still real.

As a gesture to myself and to the awareness that I couldn't continue living like that, I slowly started the process of picking up or throwing away the wreckage I had found temporary consolation in. Bit by bit, day by day, I took out newspapers, threw away coffee cups and paper bags, and picked up clothes.

Two things remained where I had dropped them the afternoon of the eleventh: the pants and shoes I had worn when I went to work that morning. The shoes, a pair of brown loafers that had been polished to a solid shine and that had still looked like new, were now scuffed and scraped to a degree that no amount of polish could conceal.

The pair of pants I had been wearing were intact, except for a slight tear on one of the legs and a few black marks. I couldn't believe that they didn't have any blood on them, particularly when I had knelt to help the man with the head wound. I knew that I would never wear those pants again—or the pair of shoes. Weirdly, I had put the shirt I had been wearing in the dirty clothes basket when I took it off and forgotten all about it. I can't even remember now what shirt I wore. But the shoes and pants I regarded as souvenirs of what I lived through.

I took a nine-by-twelve FedEx box, which was among the trash that had accumulated, and ceremoniously placed the shoes inside. I took the pants and put them atop the shoes. I closed the box and placed it on the top shelf of my closet, knowing that, at least for now, I planned on keeping these clothes with me forever. I didn't think I would ever want to look at them again. But, for whatever reason, I just couldn't throw them away. They represented too much to me. They were the only physical reminders of my place in that day. If, years from now, my memories became hazy, my feelings detached, I could take the box from wherever it would be at that time, open it, and touch the items to feel and remember that beautifully blue morning.

"Ground Zero"

I didn't want to go back downtown, back to what was now being called "Ground Zero." I was already down there every day in my mind. But eventually, the time came when the office building downtown was ready, and we were scheduled to return, and simply put, I didn't want fear to be my reason for not returning.

Because I didn't know how I would react, on November 10, the Saturday before we were to return, I decided to go down to Ground Zero … by myself. It was early, around seven in the morning. It was another beautiful day. I stood on the corner of Broadway and Fulton, outside my office building. There were barricades blocking entry onto Fulton Street from Broadway. One could look at Ground Zero only from that vantage point a block away.

Looking at Building Number 5 of the World Trade Center or, rather, the blackened, charred remains of it, I did what came so naturally those days. I started crying. I had my head down, and I felt an arm go around my shoulders. I looked up, and it was a policeman. He tightened his hold on me and said, "Let it out." I put my head on his shoulder and wept.

Another officer came up to us, and as I composed myself, they talked with me. I told them about my personal experience of that day. They both were incredibly consoling, and I felt very comfortable with them—comfortable enough to ask if they might let me into Ground Zero, to stand where I had stood the morning of 9/11 on Church Street. One of them went to speak with his superior and then came back and said, "Just follow us."

The two officers led me through security, and past the barriers, and we walked down Fulton Street to Church Street, the street I had been on during most of the attack—the street where I had watched all those people fall to their deaths—the street I was on when the second plane hit—the street from which I had to run for my life.

Ground Zero was still a massive field of ruin and wreckage, smoke still rising from the remains, toxins in the air. Every emotion I had felt on 9/11 came rushing back to me.

But, I also felt a new emotion. One of appreciation for being able to stand there. I considered it a gift—a gift to be able to acknowledge, honor, and show my respect to all those courageous victims of that morning. Standing there, I thought about and accepted having been part of that day. I took in the whole scope of the site. Only a small segment of the façade of the North Tower—the tower I had tried to run to, wanting to do something—remained standing. I told the officers about my attempt to get to the tower that morning and pointed out to them where I had to turn back. They assured me I had probably saved my own life by doing that.

We stayed about fifteen to twenty minutes. When it was time to go, I asked for just a moment alone, and they graciously stepped back a bit. I took my final moment with the site, kneeling among the spirits of those who had died, with the gratitude that I was alive. I had brought six roses with me. I laid them down, knowing they wouldn't remain there long. But for that moment, I had contributed something beautiful to that place of tragedy and loss. It was enough.

Past security and back out on the corner of Broadway and Fulton, the officers and I said our goodbyes, and they stuck out their hands to shake mine. I, instead, hugged each of them and told them that I considered them my angels that morning. Two angels in blue.

I left them and walked back to the Chambers Street subway entrance, crying again, but now I cried with a serenity and feeling of gratitude toward my Higher Power, the world, and the universe for the gift of having just stood on hallowed ground.

November 12

That next Monday, November 12, we started working back at our building, two months and one day since the terrorist attack. November 12—the morning Flight 587 crashed in Queens.

As soon as we received the first interoffice email that morning about the crash of Flight 587, I realized that life was no longer as it had been on September 10. As everyone waited for further developments about the crash, it seemed so strange to be hoping it had been an accident.

The crash rekindled all the fears, all the feelings we had been experiencing for the past two months. Television carried familiar images of burning debris, rescue workers carrying draped corpses, firefighters, and police staggering out of the devastation, gasping for air. It brought it all back.

Each morning as I arrived at Chambers Street, the smell of smoke was present as soon as the doors of the subway cars opened. Coming up onto the street, the smell was even stronger above ground, and I breathed it all in—the smoke and whatever toxins remained in it.

Barricades now blocked certain streets. As I walked toward Ground Zero, the number of police and the soldiers in uniform with their guns suggested a military state, a city torn apart by war. As I would walk the blocks to my office building, I'd pass the still smoldering ruins of Ground Zero. And in the air floated the tiny particles of toxins and hazardous chemicals and ashes of those who had died, which we breathed into our lungs. It would be years yet before it came to light just how unhealthy it was for all of us who spent any significant time down there.

St. Paul's Church, next to my office building, was being used as a relief center for those protecting the sacred site and for those who worked among the ruins of what was now a huge burial ground. St. Paul's had become an improvised memorial to those who were gone. The high, black wrought-iron fence in front of the church was adorned with tributes—a huge card made by a grade-school class in the Midwest, photos of victims, and draped sheets covered with signatures and messages of condolence from those who came by. Flowers, candles, and personal mementos were left behind.

Early in the morning, crowds would start to gather, to stand in silence, to see for themselves, to try to take it in. But I winced each time I saw a camera being held up. I labeled all those who gathered from early morning to early evening as tourists, there only to gawk and stare at something that I felt the need to protect. I wanted to yell at them, the parents with their children, the young kids pointing and staring. I know now that I used them as an outlet for the anger that was inside me. A pent-up anger that I needed to direct at someone, anyone. Not until I took my own parents there did I realize the significance and importance of others visiting the site.

Thanksgiving

My folks were finally able to come to the city. They came to be with me on Thanksgiving. I would usually have spent it at their home in Pennsylvania or at Sue's home in Maryland, the whole family together. But this year, I was part of a much larger family. I belonged to this city, and we had just suffered a terrible loss. I couldn't leave it. To do so would have been like deserting my blood family after the loss of a loved one. I didn't think I would want to be with anyone that Thanksgiving. I thought I'd prefer to be alone, not knowing what the day or the city would be like for me. But my parents, being parents and sometimes knowing better than I, drove in to be with me, just for the day.

When they arrived very early Thanksgiving Day, I asked them if they wanted to go to Ground Zero. Though they had their hesitations about whether to go, they did feel it was important to see it. And I found it important for me to show it to them.

We took a cab down. The crowds were already in place, even by early morning on a holiday. I could see, from my parents' expressions as we got out of the cab, that they were already taken aback by what they saw. We walked to St. Paul's, next to my building, to the now even busier relief center. I stood back and let them take it in on their own.

I watched my dad sign one of the sheets hanging there, putting his private thoughts down in words. As I watched him, my mom came over to me, tears in her eyes, and simply said, "This is so sad."

I walked them to one of the barricades and pointed out to them what had happened and where I had been. My hands shook; my voice trembled. A woman next to us looked at me. One of my parents told her I had been there that day. The woman reached over and took my hand.

I then took them into my office building and up to the offices, which were empty. We walked into the offices that looked down on Ground Zero, a view few people had the opportunity to see. It made the destruction even more devastating to take in.

Once leaving my building, we walked a few blocks that still gave an indication that life was different. My dad tripped over a fire hose and fell. He later found out that fall had torn his rotator cuff.

We ended up having our Thanksgiving dinner that afternoon at a diner in my neighborhood. We each had the turkey special. It was a lot of food. It was a Thanksgiving I will never forget.

My Own Leap

Every morning, as soon as I came up onto the street from the subway to head to my office, I would start to cry. My anxiety was palpable as I had to pass the burned-out shell of Building Number 5 (where my favorite bookstore had been) and the remaining ruins and rubble of Ground Zero. After my first full week of work, I felt emotionally burned-out, exhausted, and weary. I spent most of that weekend sleeping.

Each day, I had to walk past what had once been the World Trade Center and be reminded that it was gone. The enjoyment I felt each morning as I would head to work was eradicated, replaced with dread. I mostly stayed in our office building once I got to work. It made the lunchtimes I once looked forward to each noontime notably challenging. If I hadn't had time to make my lunch, I would hurriedly leave the building to buy something and dash back inside to eat it.

I didn't want to look toward where I had eaten my lunches on so many days in the past. There was no longer a plaza. No fountain. No sculptured sphere. Now it was nothing but a vestige—a pile of scorched ruins and skeletal remains that were still smoldering.

Each day, once I was inside my office, I could do my job as efficiently as before. I could laugh with my coworkers and make a random joke about something. We would talk but usually not about that day when our lives changed. It was too painful for most and easier to just evade the subject entirely.

But as each workday passed and I sat doing my work, I couldn't avoid thinking about it. Thinking of everyone who had died that fateful morning. I couldn't stop thinking of them because their deaths were leading me to reexamine my life. And under the glaring spotlight of the truth, I saw myself as a person defined by his job and his sobriety. I felt grateful that I had been able to hold on to my sobriety but began to question my job. The thing I had loved the most about it was working by the World Trade Center. Now it was just a job I went to every day, always filled with uneasiness and dread. I couldn't imagine continuing like that for the rest of my life.

My life had been taken on 9/11—the life I knew. I needed to discover who I was now. I was no longer the Artie of the tenth of September 2001. Though I walked away from the rubble with my life (for which I'm grateful), the person inside me died. I had yet to be reborn. I was still sifting through the pieces of who I once was. I had been afraid of going back downtown to work, but I did it. Now I had to face the fears of moving forward with my life, which, for me, meant I had to leave my job.

The Monday of my third week back at work, which was the week after Thanksgiving, I gave my notice. That Friday was to be my last day.

I was ready to leave a job I had had for thirteen years. A job that was never a career I had planned on. It became a job that was uncomplicated and safe, with a good salary, benefits, paid vacation, 401(k) plans—all the things that, for many, define success. Remember, originally, I had planned to stay at this job for a year or two. How quickly those thirteen years flew by. I didn't want another thirteen to go by in a blink of an eye.

My viewpoint of life changed the instant I went through the revolving door of my office building's lobby on September 11 and stepped into the ankle-deep paper covering Dey Street. I witnessed the deaths of too many people that day, many of them the people I watched descend the length of the towers. I still think of that one moment in which they all had to decide for themselves how their lives would end. They had to choose how to die. They took that leap.

I was one of the fortunate ones. I walked away from the rubble that morning. But I now faced my own decision. How would I live the rest of this life I'd been graciously given? I must choose how to live. I had to take my own leap.

Into the Unknown

I was unemployed, but having been diagnosed with PTSD early on, I was able to collect disability, and I didn't have to worry about finances for a while. Instead of trying to decide right away what I should do next with my life, I continued doing what I had been doing, which was write. Every day, I'd write about what it was like to be in a city that was still grieving. I wrote about my own grief and other emotions. I wrote mostly for myself, but I also sent emails to friends and family at the time. Continuing to write led me to the next new chapter in my life—a chapter that never would have happened had I not taken that leap of my own.

It was January 2002. The city was still dealing with the grief of 9/11, as was I. Down at Ground Zero, the search and rescue had long stopped. Now it was all about taking away the charred remains of what once was.

Even though it was a new year, neither I nor the city had restored ourselves back to life as it was pre-9/11. No, that was impossible. Our city and its residents would never be the same again. One doesn't heal overnight (if at all), especially from what we had lived through. Families who had lost someone were still grieving. Fire departments, police stations, and EMS units that had lost one or more of their members grieved as well, all the while having to carry on with protecting the public as always. And those of us who survived that day and didn't lose anyone we personally knew had to grieve over the loss of ourselves—of who we used to be before 9/11—because we could never, and would never, go back to who we once were.

An Idea

One morning, I was walking to my noontime twelve-step meeting. On my way there, out of nowhere, I had the thought *I wonder if all I've been putting down on paper these past months could be a play.*

It surprised me the idea even entered my mind because I had given up being part of the theater community those many years ago, back in 1988. But once the seed of that idea broke through, my thoughts and my imagination started feeding it.

I felt it was important for someone who survived the terrorist attack to share what it was like to live through that atrocity with people who hadn't been physically present. I knew I wanted to tell my story. Not because it was of any greater significance than any others', but I immediately regarded this as a way for me to pay tribute to all who died. And it could also be my contribution to help ensure that we never forget.

As the seedling of the idea began to sprout, I knew it would be a one-man play and, since it was my story, I wanted to be the one telling it. I never in my imagination thought I would go back on a stage. But now I had a reason to. I also knew what I would call the play, the title blossoming out of nowhere: *That Day in September.*

To keep myself in check and make sure this was an idea worth pursuing, I decided to speak to my friend, Richard Masur, a fine and respected actor. I told him of what I had been thinking and asked if he'd read all I'd written and give me his honest opinion about my words becoming the foundation of a one-man play. So, I printed out all I had and took it to Richard. He called me that same night and said he thought it would make a very good play and, in fact, he'd like to direct it.

Suddenly, just a passing thought seemed to be headed to becoming a reality. I had the words for the beginning of a script, a title for the play, and a director. Now, the work would begin to bring this all to fruition.

The Work Begins

Richard and I began the task of taking all I had written and shaping it into a rough draft of a play. We discussed whether I should do the piece on stage or we should have an actor do it. Fortunately, Richard felt the same as I did and thought I should perform in it. But *performing* wasn't the correct word because I wouldn't be acting out a role. This was going to be me on stage as myself, telling my personal story and not reciting words about a made-up story, which was all the more reason Richard felt it important that I tell it. It was my story to tell.

I was more than aware of the irony in all this. I had moved to New York to be on the stage. I gave it all up, and then the most horrific event I'd ever lived through would now be putting me back on the stage. Certainly a detour on my life's journey I had not expected. And an example of life going in a complete circle.

The initial draft was me just telling the details of 9/11 in chronological order as I witnessed them. I did this in a series of individual monologues, which came across as me just reporting on the day, like a newscaster. Richard felt the script needed a more personal touch. He thought that for the audience to truly connect with my story, they should get to know who I was first and foremost. He thought it would make what I went through on 9/11 more impactful and help the audience realize the extent of the horror of that morning's events. I originally wasn't sure because I didn't know how much to reveal about myself.

I never held back the fact that I was gay. I had hidden in shame for far too many years and swore I would never be ashamed of who I was as a gay man, so I didn't mind sharing that. What I wasn't sure about was being open about my addictions. The whole purpose behind twelve-step programs is the anonymity factor. But, I had gotten pulled out of the whirlpool of addiction, and if my admission could help an audience member, then even more reason to talk about my struggles with both my sexuality and my addictions. And Richard pointed out the more the audience knew about what my life had been like before 9/11, the more they could understand the changes 9/11 brought about in my view of life now.

I decided he was right and figured I might as well go full steam ahead and not hold back the ugliness of my life. So, my sexuality and spirituality and addiction were now part of the script.

After our first public reading of the play, it was those aspects of the script that many people commented on, saying they made the whole story more meaningful.

That First Public Reading

That first public reading took place in August 2002. During the time leading up to that, aside from editing and reworking the script, I was emailing theaters and producers across the country, hoping someone would be willing to take a chance on an unknown playwright and a yet-to-be-produced play.

As for the stage reading, the evening's performance would simply be me on a stool, a music stand in front of me with the script on it. And in that way, *That Day in September* would be heard for the first time.

I felt tangible excitement the night of the first public reading. I was off stage but could hear the volume of voices increase as the seats filled up. My parents and Sue were in the audience.

When it was time, the lights went to black, and I walked out and took my place on the stool. I took a deep breath. The spotlight came up and I began.

It was a small space, and as I got further into my story, I could easily hear muffled crying coming from the audience. So, I at least knew people were being moved by my story and the words I had chosen to tell it.

At the end, the lights came up, and I could see people wiping their eyes and blowing their noses. The applause sounded like it was coming from a crowd of five hundred. The night was a success, meaning the script had done what I hoped it would. It told my story and touched people.

The Next Step

While working on the script, I continued working on finding a theater for the play to premiere at. Through Google, I searched for every professional theater and producer in the States. I sent countless emails to each theater and producer, telling them about my play and asking if they might be interested in it.

A producer in LA contacted me almost as soon as he had gotten my email. Though he didn't have a theater, he was interested in finding one and producing the play. So, I kept him up to date with the progress of editing and revising the script while he sought out a theater.

He happened upon a small black-box theater in Hollywood that was known for presenting plays and musicals with central themes about the gay experience. Though *That Day in September* was by no means a "gay play," I think the fact that I was gay and included some of my coming-out story in the script appealed to the theater. The dates for the run of the show were September 21 through October 20.

Before the opening at the theater, though, I planned to preview the piece at California Lutheran University for two evenings, September 19 and 20, the equivalent of an out-of-town tryout.

The biggest problem I had to face was how I would get to California. Flying out there wasn't an option for me at that time. It was too soon to put myself on an airplane. The very thought unnerved me and made me extremely anxious. In fact, as I write this, I've yet to fly. I don't know what that will be like for me when the time comes when I have no other choice but to board a plane.

Since air travel was out of the question, and since I had no car, the only alternative was travel by rail. So, I traveled by train across the country, from New York to Los Angeles. It was one of the most enjoyable experiences I've had. I had my own private compartment, and when dining, I would always sit with different people at the tables of four. I met interesting people, and when they found out why I was traveling to California, they were full of questions about my 9/11 experience, sharing with me their own accounts of where they had been and how they found out about the towers being hit. I would suggest that anyone experience seeing our country by train. I saw vistas of postcard quality.

Of course, before boarding that train, before doing the play in Hollywood, the first anniversary of 9/11 came. To be honest, I have absolutely no recollection of how I observed that all-important day. I know I didn't go to any events that took place at Ground Zero. Since quitting my job, I had no reason, or desire, to go back there. I'm sure I went to my twelve-step meeting, maybe saw my therapist, surely spoke with my parents. And I'm sure I spent a good part of that day crying.

LA

I won't be mentioning the name of the theater in Hollywood or the producer of my play, because, unfortunately, it was probably the worst experience I've had as an actor. Neither the producer nor the theater did much preparation for the play. Little to no advertising. No interviews set up. I can give them credit for getting the *Los Angeles Times* and a premiere West Hollywood gay magazine to review the play, so I was fortunate in that regard. Both publications gave the play a favorable review. But even with good word in print, our audiences were small. They didn't have room in their budget for newspaper, radio, or television advertisement, and the run of the play was too short to build up good word of mouth.

But all that disappointment was minimal when I was finally in front of an audience (no matter the size). Richard directed the show very minimally. Like in that initial reading, I simply sat on a stool with a music stand in front of me holding the script. Though I had the play memorized, we did it as a reading, with lighting used for changes in mood during the monologues.

More rewarding than any applause was greeting the people who would wait for me at the stage door after each performance. I could see in their faces that my story had touched them. The comment I heard the most was that my words made that day much more real for them, as they were on the other side of the country that day in September. Their words of appreciation, often accompanied by tears, made up for the underperformance of the theater management.

And, I learned a valuable lesson from those audience members who would wait for me after the play. Inevitably, each person I took the time to speak with always ended up telling me the story of where he or she was on 9/11. Granted, most of them were in LA, but they still had a story. They told me where they were when they first heard the news, where they watched the images on TV in horror. The lesson for me, from them, was the realization that all of us, of a certain age, have a story of 9/11. Mine just happens to be that I was there in New York as an eyewitness. But that doesn't negate all the stories from all over the world, because it was, indeed, a global event. A catastrophic act of terrorism that affected everyone everywhere.

Everyone has a story of 9/11.

Back to New York

When the play ended, I left California with a sense of accomplishment, having done what I set out to do: simply tell my story and touch some lives by giving people a deeper understanding of what it was like the morning of 9/11.

In the same manner that I had arrived, I left Los Angeles by train, crossing once again this magnificent country of ours.

I need to take a moment here to tell you what I've often told other people. The two years that I would end up spending working on *That Day in September* (2002–2003) were the most fulfilling years I've ever experienced in my life. I was doing something important. I was touching people's lives and giving them a glimpse into the day when everything changed. And I did this as selflessly as possible. My motivation was never to fuel my ego but to do what small part I could to help ensure we, as a country, would never forget.

That said, once back in New York, Richard and I set about doing some editing and taking out some of the material and putting in some new. While Richard and I did some more work on the script, we hoped for a run of the show somewhere in the city.

After a series of rewrites and edits, we found a small black box of a theater, which I, putting up my own money, booked for a week of performances. It was still me on the stool, with the music stand and script, but we now wanted to get reactions from New Yorkers.

Our advertising consisted of emailing the theater email list and my own list of friends and family. My parents surprised me by coming to see the opening night performance. They came to surprise me, but my mom had a distinctive cough. As I stood backstage, I heard that cough and peaked through the side curtain. There they were, Mom and Dad, in the front row. I was so touched that they had come.

One night, a group of the lawyers I had worked with came. And each performance had a sizable audience (which wasn't difficult to obtain considering the tiny space of the theater).

Then at one of the performances, much to my surprise, was Karen, the girl I moved to New York with. She was now a theatrical producer and somehow had heard about my play and that I was performing it. To say it was a surprise to have her there would be a huge understatement. We greeted each other with a hug in the lobby after the performance. She suggested we go for coffee, so we went to a diner around the corner from the theater.

After much catching up on each other's lives, Karen, who had produced quite a few Off-Broadway shows at the Lamb's Theatre (where I had performed that Christmas children's play that got me to New York), said she would be interested in producing *That Day in September* in their own black-box theater.

Talk about life coming full circle. And talk about a dream coming true. I'd always wanted to perform in an Off-Broadway play. And now I would be. And in a play that I wrote.

Off-Broadway

It was 2003 when Karen and I had that coffee and conversation about her producing *That Day in September*. The Lamb's Theatre had a lovely ninety-nine-seat black-box theater, which was a perfect venue for the play. This would be a fully mounted Off-Broadway production, with a minimal set (that Richard Masur designed), as well as back-screen projections and audio and lighting effects.

Of course, it would have made sense to wait to open the play during September. But I was anxious to get it up and running during the summer, as was Karen. The only hindrance was that Karen would be in Italy when the play would open on July 15. We debated back and forth if we should go ahead and open the play without Karen being present. In hindsight, I wish we had waited for her to return from Italy before opening the play. We might have had a more successful run if we had.

The play was produced on a shoestring budget, so we were limited as far as advertisements went. We hoped reviews might make up for that, but none of the major newspapers sent reviewers to see the play (which I still don't understand why). Some second stringers or trade newspapers reviewed the play, and the reviews were mixed. Some felt I wanted to profit from the tragedy, which, of all the criticisms, hurt the most because that was the furthest from the truth.

But we got good-sized audiences, and after each performance, I would experience the same reactions from the audience members that I got in LA. They would express their gratitude and would end up sharing their own 9/11 stories with me. It was in moments like that when I truly believed in what I was doing and wanted to continue to do it as long as possible.

My dream was to spend at least the next five years traveling the country with the play. And there was some interest expressed in that happening. In fact, despite the mixed reviews, one of the major premium cable channels expressed interest, and a meeting was set up with me and an agent from a prestigious talent agency. Also, an independent producer expressed interest in seeing if the play could tour the country. All very exciting to me, of course. It would be another dream come true.

We had decided on a limited run of the play to see how it would do. And, after the first few weeks, attendance began to drop off. There wasn't enough word of mouth getting out there. And, as I mentioned, we didn't have an extravagant budget to advertise with. Perhaps this is just me wanting to soothe my disappointment and bruised ego, but I think it was still too early for a play about 9/11 to be on a New York stage. The wounds were still fresh and the healing continuing.

Karen returned from Italy a few weeks after we opened, and she wasn't able to save what had become a sinking ship. She had to make the painful decision to end the run of the play earlier than planned. A play closing early meant it wasn't a success, and suddenly, I found all the doors that had begun to open slam shut.

The agent no longer returned my calls. The cable channel was no longer interested. And the producer who was going to help me take the play on the road changed his mind. It was a dark period for me. As I explained, the two years I had spent on *That Day in September* were the most fulfilling years of my life. And now that fulfillment was gone. I felt it still important to share my story but had, at that time, no means to do so.

There really was no one to blame for how things had worked out. There is a saying within the twelve-step community: "Just do the next right thing." I tried to put that pearl of wisdom to use and believe that the play closing was "the next right thing" to happen. But there had to be a next step, right? A new "next right thing"? Well, it turned out that there was. And it came to me one day as I was walking to my AA meeting in late August 2003.

I would move to Lancaster, Pennsylvania.

Lancaster?

I never thought I'd leave New York. I assumed I would take my dying breath there. I loved the city. I loved being a New Yorker. I always felt amused (and somewhat proud) when relatives or family friends back home in Maryland would ask me how life was in the big city, as if my being a New Yorker was something to be in awe of.

So, when, out of nowhere, I had the thought to leave the city and move to Lancaster, I was just as shocked as my New York friends were when I told them.

But 9/11 had shifted my priorities, and suddenly, family was now at the top of my list of what was truly important. That was the one and only good thing I could personally pull from the wreckage of 9/11 at that time.

For twenty-six years, I had seen my folks maybe three or four times a year. I now wanted to see them more than that. Being near them was not a desire but a necessity. Perhaps, if one were to analyze it, I wanted to feel that safety of "home," even though Lancaster, Pennsylvania, wasn't my hometown. My parents represented home for me now. And I wanted, and needed, to be with them. To be home. I wanted to make up for all that lost time when I didn't see them during my twenty-six years in New York.

Though I felt confident that moving to Pennsylvania was the next right thing for me to do, it wasn't without conflict. It had only been two years since 9/11, and in many ways, I felt the city was still mourning and recovering. By leaving, I felt as if I was deserting a friend in need. But, even with those conflicted feelings swirling in my head, I knew it was the right thing to do. So, within a month from the moment I had the thought, I was ready to leave New York.

I needed to see Ground Zero one last time before leaving. I don't know if it was to say goodbye or to pay my respects. It was probably both. A friend from AA went down with me. By then, a viewing platform had been erected on Fulton and Church Streets, where one could stand and see the whole of Ground Zero. We stood there, looking down at the ruins that had yet to be totally cleared away, and I just started crying. I cried because I was leaving. This was my goodbye, and my tears were filled with sorrow and grief.

After that final farewell at Ground Zero, I began packing my belongings, and in just a matter of days, friends helped me put the boxes into a U-Haul, along with a few pieces of furniture. I drove away from my apartment building and the memories of my neighborhood.

I drove out of the city through the Lincoln Tunnel and never looked back.

Pennsylvania

It was October 8, 2003, when I arrived in Millersville, a small university town outside Lancaster, where my parents lived. I stayed with them until I could find an apartment, a car, and a job.

In New York, finding an apartment one could afford was nearly impossible. But here in the surrounding areas of Lancaster, there was one apartment complex after another. My last apartment in New York was a studio apartment, one room with a tiny separate kitchen and bathroom. The apartment I found in Millersville was a one-bedroom apartment with a washer and dryer (no more weekly trips to a Laundromat), a dining room, a kitchen with a dishwasher, and a huge living room. It felt like a mansion to me. And my rent was only $600, compared to the $1,200 I'd been paying for my studio in New York.

I also quickly bought a used car–a Saturn–my first car in twenty-six years.

And, after going to a job fair, I was offered a job with a human services organization, which I took. I stayed at that job about a year, until I found a job I really liked and stayed at for twelve years, which was working in the box office of a professional theater in downtown Lancaster.

The only downside to this move, aside from leaving the city I loved, was I pretty much wiped out what was left in my 401(k) plan from my law firm job. That, and relying on credit cards, soon put me in debt over the years, which I only recently was able to pay off.

But, the upside to the move was that I was now near my parents. The downside mentioned here paled in comparison.

Each day after work, I would drive to my parents' and eat dinner with them. I know that it thrilled my mother to finally be able to feed her son (as if I'd been starving all those years in New York). But I didn't mind. I found it wonderful to eat her delicious home-cooked meals after years of takeout, fast food, restaurants, slices of pizza, and, when I was in the mood to cook, pots of Stovetop stuffing.

From Play to Book

Though I now lived far from New York, the city and the friends I left behind were often on my mind. And though I was where I thought I should be and where I wanted to be, I still felt guilty, feeling I had abandoned the city, which, even two years later, was still healing from the losses it had endured. I now had to grieve over and heal from 9/11 from afar, away from my fellow New Yorkers.

I needed a distraction. The two previous years of writing and performing my play had given me confidence that I was doing something important by telling my story, and it had become my heart's passion. I needed to put that passion into something. I wanted to continue to tell my story.

As with other life-changing ideas I've had in the past, one day, I just had the thought of telling my story in a book. I had all the source material I needed: my play. I decided to adapt my play into a book, calling it *That Day in September* as well.

I spent close to a year doing research on self-publishing, learning as much as I could about the smartest, and most economical, way to go about it. Once I found the publisher I wanted to go with, I began the arduous task of adapting my play into a book format. That's the thing with self-publishing; all the work, from the cover to the fonts to the appearance of each page, falls on the author. But I didn't mind. It gave me, like my play did in New York, a distraction.

Not long after my move, some symptoms of my PTSD began to invade my life, starting with the nightmares. My dreams were seldom of the event of 9/11 itself (though there were exceptions) but of some other kind of destruction. Many nights, I would dream that I was privy to information that something catastrophic was about to happen and I was trying to warn people, but they just ignored me. At times, it was the day before 9/11, and I somehow knew it was going to happen, but as with my other dreams of attempted warnings, no one would listen to me. Other dreams would have me in the middle of a disaster, filling me with fear. These nightmares caused me to start sleeping with a light on again. But those intrusive dreams came, despite the light.

PTSD

I thought I had been doing so well in dealing with my PTSD diagnosis, but what I believe I had really been doing the past two years was suppressing or denying the symptoms or both. The previous two years, which I had devoted to writing my play and sharing my story on stage, helped me, but perhaps they also distracted me from dealing with all the nightmarish memories, pain, guilt, and suffering of what I had lived through. Though I certainly put my experience of 9/11 front and center, talking about it so freely and easily each night on stage, I regarded it more as a rehearsed story to tell the audiences in front of me.

Oh, I had some performances where the safety of repeating my written words wasn't strong enough to keep some emotion at bay. I had times on stage that I would feel the tears start to come. In those times, I just went with the emotions (whatever they were). Some nights, I told my story on stage through choking tears.

Once I felt settled in Pennsylvania, I knew I needed to continue seeing a therapist. I began looking for one. I had to go through a couple of therapists before one of them unselfishly suggested a therapist who worked with people with PTSD. That's how I found Stephanie, whom I worked with for years and who helped me beyond measure. And not just with my PTSD issues. She was there for other minor and major crises that would arise in my day-to-day living. That's the thing with having PTSD. Aside from having to live with that disorder, you must deal with the common ups and downs of everyday living.

My parents were beginning to have medical issues that put me on an emotional roller coaster at times. Living near my parents, I was aware, on almost a daily basis, that they were aging. I know that's what is supposed to happen, but to see it as it progressed was difficult.

And I tried not to make them aware of my struggles with PTSD. I didn't want to go to them when I was feeling bad or depressed or having flashbacks because they had their own nightmare memories of 9/11, as they had waited to find out on that day that I was okay.

But even though I thought I managed to mask the pain and sorrow from them, I found out they were aware after all. They were my parents. They knew me well and could see the changes in my personality that were the results of living through 9/11.

One night, I was driving to their house for dinner, and images of 9/11 started flashing across my mind. I burst out crying—sobbing, really, while trying to drive. As I neared their house, I made myself stop crying and mentally prepared myself to act as if I was fine. But the minute I walked into their house, I just broke down in tears. My mom ran over to me, hugged me, and asked what was wrong. Had I had an accident? Did I hit somebody?

Through gasps, I said no, it was 9/11. My dad took me to the couch and held me while I sobbed and spoke aloud of the images I was seeing, mostly people falling to their deaths. My mom sat down beside me, upset now herself, and they both comforted me.

Once I could compose myself, we sat down to try to eat. It was then my parents told me that I couldn't hide things from them. They could read my emotional scale and knew if I was having a good or bad day. They knew I was a changed person.

I didn't have such supportive understanding from all family members. One thing that was very hard for me was being around groups of people, even family. I found it exhausting to put on the pretense that I was having a good day if I wasn't.

When the whole family would gather at my parents' house (which included Sue, my niece and nephew, and their spouses and children), I would find that noise and general commotion a bit overwhelming. It could easily take me back to the chaos and calamity of 9/11. As with most families, everyone would congregate in the kitchen. I'd often go into the living room and sit on the couch, and my head would soon fall back, and I'd be asleep. I was aware I was doing it, because it felt safe. Or I sometimes would just go into my bedroom, if I was having a really bad day, and nap.

Sleep took me away from everything for the moment. From the noise, which would take back to me the sounds of sirens and screams. The number of people in the house at one time would remind me of running with crowds of strangers for our lives.

One family member, in anger, made the comment to me that all I did was sleep when they were there visiting. I knew I had no way of getting that person to the point of understanding why that was. This is one commonality among 9/11 survivors. No one can ever truly understand.

In My Solitude

PTSD might manifest itself in one individual differently than it does in someone else. I had the obvious indicators that I was suffering from PTSD while some other symptoms were unique to me. And these symptoms didn't come to the surface all at one time. It was a slow progression. A progression of me allowing the emotions of the trauma of 9/11 to make themselves known to me, proving that I had indeed been changed the day I stepped out onto the street in front of the Twin Towers.

I spent many hours crying in Stephanie's office, which I considered my safe place. I trusted her and felt at ease with her. Her gentle way of working with me helped me know I could reveal anything to her, some things I had never told anyone before. I could be raw and real with her.

The one obvious change in me was the least obvious to me. I had become a loner, hermit-like almost. My daily routine consisted of going to work, then to my parents' for dinner, then home to the sanctuary of my apartment. I had left my apartment in Millersville in 2005 and now lived over a funeral home in a spacious apartment for an extremely reasonable rent in the city of Lancaster. I see the irony now that I lived over a funeral home. It put me close to death every day. Fortunately, I didn't have to go through the funeral home to get to my apartment. There were outside stairs. But I couldn't help but know that on the floors below me were coffins and bodies laid to rest.

Stephanie called this apartment "my cave," because I lived as if I was hiding from the outside world within the welcome confines of the walls that surrounded me. I would sit in my living room on the couch nightly watching Netflix.

I did take steps to socialize. I would, at times, do things with my coworkers. I began to meet other people but found it hard to make friends with them. When first meeting someone and making small talk, it usually would come up that I had moved to the area from New York City. People would ask me if I was there during 9/11. When I told them just how close I was to it, I could see a look in their eyes that I read as "Oh no, what do I say now?" An awkwardness would follow, so I would change the subject, mostly to put them at ease. It got to where I would try to avoid the subject of 9/11 coming up, so others wouldn't feel uncomfortable.

What I longed for, though, was for someone to respond with "What was that like for you?" or questions along those lines. I wanted people to ask if I'd mind talking about it. I wanted, and needed, to talk about it. I wouldn't have minded. It was now part of my backstory.

I was also meeting other members of the gay community. I'd make myself arrange meetings for dinner or coffee to be sociable. Though this might be hard to understand, I felt other gay people from here just didn't "get" me—my New York demeanor and attitude, my jokes, my gossip, my acknowledgment of and love for anything to do with the theater or movies. It made me miss my gay friends back in New York terribly. But I had to understand that I had histories with each of my friends back there. I had made most of my good friendships while in my thirties, just as I was getting my feet wet living publicly and without shame as a gay man. Those were the friends who supported and encouraged me when I decided to come out to my parents. I lived through the AIDS crisis with them, losing one of my dearest friends to that illness.

I did meet a couple from New York, who now lived in Lancaster. Now they "got" me. All the things I mentioned as obstacles were absent when around those two guys. They both came from theater backgrounds. They knew all the obsolete names I'd bring up. They knew who Julie Budd was! We'd laugh. Have game nights. Watch the Tonys together. I did spend a fair amount of time with them. But that all ended when they decided to move to New Jersey.

And me?

I retreated into my cave.

2011

I live with an unwelcome companion of sorrow, but I have found ways to do some good, now living with, and loving, my parents and sharing my story whenever and wherever I can.

Since the beginning of 2011, some significant things had happened that had been drawing me out of the bleakness I once found comfort in. And, as usual, I don't know whether to attribute these things to fate or circumstance or God. Perhaps there's no need for me to know.

In the beginning of 2011, my parents were each facing medical issues. I needed to find a new apartment, and since my folks lived in a two-bedroom home, it seemed sensible for me to move in with them and to begin acting as a caregiver and helper. It was the best decision we three ever came to. I could be present for them now that they especially needed me. We certainly went through a roller coaster of emotions when it came to illnesses. But now they had me to do the heavy lifting.

In January, after years of searching, I found a whole network of 9/11 survivors that I connected with online. I found comfort in having people I could write or talk to who I knew fully understood what I was saying or feeling. I realized I was not alone; there are so many of us.

And, I was so very fortunate to have found Stephanie.

I'm not sure what I think when it comes to the timing of moments in one's life. I don't know if I can believe that things happen when they're supposed to. Or that everything happens for a reason. If there is a spiritual or cosmic connection to how the circumstances of our lives play out, I don't understand it. I had asked myself these questions over the past years as I've tried to understand how, and why, the events of 9/11 happened, and why I survived and others didn't.

I couldn't ignore, though, what had transpired over three months of 2011.

The year before had been difficult emotionally, as if I had only now allowed myself to fully grieve and mourn over all that was lost the morning of 9/11. Maybe I hadn't been ready to express just how deep the sorrow inside me was until then, as the tenth anniversary approached.

It's terribly lonely living in a city where no one else knows what it was like to be in New York City on 9/11. As much as they might try, no one can truly know what I go through each day. I did have Stephanie, and she at least understood the effects of post-traumatic stress, so that was helpful. Her office was a refuge for me.

And as I've written before, I didn't want to burden my parents with what I was going through.

For many years, after moving to Pennsylvania, I often searched for organizations or support groups for the survivors of 9/11. The only groups I could always find were for the families who lost someone. But never anything for the eyewitnesses and survivors of that day. I finally stopped looking.

And then, at the beginning of 2011, I decided to do another Google search. This time, right near the top of the results page, I found a group, Voices of September 11. Once a month, this organization provided a teleconference session for survivors, facilitated by a therapist. I readily participated in these because they were primarily for survivors who had left New York. So, I now had the opportunity to speak with other survivors for the first time.

Then, a friend from California called to tell me of a website someone had told him about: World Trade Center Survivors' Network. I quickly joined that online group, and through that, I found another survivors' support group on Facebook.

For years, I had never had contact with another survivor of 9/11, and now I was speaking with, and writing to, many of them. I can't describe the tremendous comfort and solace I received in having people in my life who knew just what I meant when I expressed a feeling or a thought, not having to explain myself. And the emails they sent could have been written by me; I found that much clarity and understanding when I read them. I sensed new friendships beginning because of the kinship we shared in our collective experiences of 9/11.

The puzzling thing was that these groups had been around for years and I was only then becoming aware of them. Stephanie suggested perhaps I hadn't been ready for them until that time. Is this yet another example of those cosmic questions I carry with me?

The Blogs

Returning to Ground Zero

Since moving to Lancaster, I hadn't been back to New York City. My excuses had been that I didn't have the money or the time. But, truth be told, the thought of going back for a visit was too overwhelming. There was a resistance on my part; an avoidance, to be sure. To go back to New York would be to go back to that day in September. I knew that if I were to go into New York, I would have to revisit Ground Zero, and I wasn't ready to do that. Life had been difficult enough living with the memories. I was afraid of reliving them if I were to go back to where they had taken place.

I'd also been oppressed with shame and guilt over having left the city, despite having a good reason to. When I left New York City, it was still recovering and healing. As irrational as it may seem, I felt I had abandoned the city, comparable to distancing myself from a family member in a time of crisis.

I did regret that I had let the memories and remorse keep me away from the city I loved for all those years, but perhaps I hadn't been ready for a return.

I finally decided to return to New York, specifically to Ground Zero. And, like my move to Lancaster, this decision took no deliberation. One day in March, after leaving a therapy session, I suddenly just knew. It was time. Stephanie and I hadn't even discussed my going back during that session, but I knew I was ready. And I knew when I wanted to make the trip back. I wanted to do this for my birthday, which was Monday, April 25, 2011. It was to be my gift to myself. It somehow seemed appropriate. And right.

Friday, April 22, my parents, my Sue, and I boarded the train in Lancaster and headed to New York.

I knew Ground Zero had become a construction site. But it was (and is) still sacred ground to me.

I wanted to stand where I stood the morning of 9/11, on Church Street.

I wanted to remember, and acknowledge, those who died.

For whatever reason, it was important to retrace my steps of that morning with my family, so they might have a better understanding of what it was like for me.

The weekend would be not about visiting the city but about reclaiming the place the city had in my life and heart. It was about returning to pay long-overdue respect to all who died.

Once we arrived in New York and checked into a hotel, we took a cab down to 195 Broadway, the office building where I was working on 9/11.

As soon as we were out of the cab and walking down Dey Street, toward Church Street, I began sobbing. Sue took my arm and walked with me, our parents a few steps behind.

Once we reached the corner of Dey and Church Streets, we stopped, and I just stood there and sobbed, my parents and her comforting me.

There was nothing there to remind me, or others, of the Twin Towers that once reached up into the heavens. It was, as I envisioned, just a construction site. But I could so vividly remember what once stood there.

I could point out to my family where I was during each moment of that horrific morning. I showed them where I stood when I first looked up at the North Tower. Where I was when the second plane hit. Where I fell. Where I ran up Fulton Street and stopped to help the injured man.

They could now visualize all I had described to them in words.

I don't know if I believe things happen when they're supposed to.

Or that everything happens for a reason.

If there is a spiritual or cosmic connection to how the circumstances of our lives play out, I don't understand it.

I do remember 2011 being difficult emotionally.

I think it was during that year that I allowed myself to begin to fully grieve and mourn all that was lost the morning of 9/11. Maybe it was the approaching tenth anniversary that year that caused me to express just how deep my sorrow was.

I began seeking out opportunities to speak about my experience. I joined the county's speakers' bureau and, through it, got to speak to senior groups and civic organizations. I also sent emails to all the middle and high schools in the county and began sharing my story with students, one of the most receptive and attentive groups I've spoken to. So, sharing my story with others is important to me, especially when sharing it with students.

People ask if it's difficult talking about it publicly. It is draining, emotionally, but also fulfilling. I want to continue to share my story with students because it is important for them to never forget. And for them to remind the generations that will follow. I want to help them always remember.

And for those fortunate enough to have yet to experience tragedy or trauma, try to remember that you never know what might be behind a person's smile. We all have our stories. And for some, our stories contain memories we wish we could forget.

On the Death of bin Laden

I witnessed the magnitude of bin Laden's evil on 9/11. My life was irreparably changed because of him.

When the news of his death became public, I sat in my apartment in downtown Lancaster watching the television, my hand to my mouth, becoming aware I was holding my breath.

I felt so isolated in the moments that followed the president's address confirming bin Laden's death. Watching the aerial shots on TV of people in New York gathering at Ground Zero made me long to be there with them. I felt so alone. I had mourned with my fellow New Yorkers in the weeks and months following 9/11, experiencing a sense of connection unlike ever before. I imagined that the people of the city assembling where the Twin Towers had once stood were sensing a connection once again, hopefully of solace perhaps and a semblance of comfort. I imagined there was a collective sense of unity among them, remembering what we felt, collectively, as a city on 9/11.

I had nowhere to go in this city of Lancaster that was now my new home. There was no Ground Zero for me to go to. People wouldn't be gathering anywhere. If I were to leave my apartment and walk the streets, I would pass very few people, Lancaster not being an active city at night. And the people I would walk by would have no idea of just how significant this night was for me, as a 9/11 survivor. And though I had family and friends I could have phoned, I didn't because I was unable to put together words that could remotely describe the emptiness of not knowing what I should be feeling.

So, I sat on my couch, anxious. Anxious because everything about 9/11 was coming at me in full force. And anxious over what the retaliation for bin Laden's death would be.

The next day, and those following, I was numb, detached from emotion. Throughout the week, I kept thinking, *Why aren't I feeling anything?*

And then six days later, I went to my weekly therapy session. The moment I sat down, all those feelings I questioned not having came pouring out, and I started sobbing.

I was crying because the memories of 9/11 were as vivid as if it had just happened. I was crying, once again, for all the lives that were lost that day, my grief as raw as it was the weeks and months after 9/11. I was crying for the world that was taken from us that day—the world where we thought we were safe. And I was crying for what was taken from me on 9/11, my enthusiasm for life replaced with a broken spirit and interminable sadness.

I cried because I was glad he was dead, and justice had been served; so they said. But, for me, the justice was too quick. His life ended too easily, too quickly. But what would have been more just? A public hanging? Have him stand before every single one of us who was there that morning along with those who lost a family member, friend, or colleague that day? And then what? Stone him? I cried because no matter what we might do to make him suffer, it wouldn't be enough. I cried because even the most horrible punishment imaginable would still not be sufficient when compared to what he did. I cried because I have never felt this much hatred toward someone. And I cried because even my hate didn't fully express all that was inside me when I thought of that man.

I cried because I'm scared. Because I know this war on terror isn't over by any means. I'm afraid for what will happen next. I fear for the city I love and am no longer living in. I fear it'll happen somewhere else, where we might least expect it. And when it does happen, I know I will have to once again relive my memories of 9/11.

I cried because, for me, nothing has changed. I still have to live every day of the rest of my life with the memories. He's dead and I'm glad. But his death didn't heal me. And I know that someone else will take his place, so I imagine that, at least for the rest of my life, I will live in fear of "what's next." I cried because I know that's what they want. I cried because we haven't won. Not yet. And I fear we might never.

The Great Sadness

On 9/11/2001, I stood in front of the World Trade Center and watched the horrors of that morning as they unfolded. My life changed forever that day, as did the country's belief that we were safe from harm.

If 9/11 hadn't happened, I probably would have never left New York City to move to Lancaster, Pennsylvania. I now know, personally, how just one moment in time can alter, forever, the path of a person's life. I don't know if those moments are fate or just happenstance. I still question if life is just composed of random occurrences with no rhyme or reason, or if God is involved in those life-changing moments.

I do cringe in anger at the suggestion of some that even 9/11 was part of "God's plan" and that all things work toward the good. There was nothing "good" about what I witnessed that morning. And the only "plan" I saw was a plan acted out at the hands of madmen.

At times, I wonder just where God was that morning. On my good days, I can say God was present in the hands of everyone who reached out to help someone else. Or in the arms of people on the streets embracing one another. And in the tears as strangers cried together.

On my bad days, I am angry that, because of the laws of the universe that God had set up, God is powerless to stop mankind from acting out the evil it's capable of. I have been stripped of the unquestioning faith I once held on to, replacing it with questions I don't have the answers for.

I have become accustomed to the inner sadness that is with me every day, as I go through the motions of living my life. I compare this sadness to an article of clothing I put on every day.

Some days, it's like a light windbreaker, images and thoughts of 9/11 in the background of my mind, allowing me to go through my day with relative calm. Then some days it's as if it is a wet, heavy, woolen overcoat that weighs me down. That is when 9/11 is in the forefront of my mind's eye. Images, emotions, and heartbreak disrupting my entire day.

When I wake up in the morning, I never know which article of clothing I'll be putting on. I might even change from the windbreaker to the overcoat several times over the course of a day. Or vice versa.

I have forgotten what it is like to be happy. Genuinely happy. That's not to say I don't experience moments of pleasure or fun, but it's never long-lasting.

I don't remember what joy feels like. I haven't felt it in all these years since 9/11. And I can't remember the last time I laughed till it hurt. Again, that's not to infer I never smile or elicit a chuckle or a grin. But I can't remember doubling over in laughter. A huge belly laugh, so loud and long that I get a stitch in my side.

This is the life for a survivor of 9/11 and perhaps a survivor of any tragedy or trauma.

That's why it is easier just to isolate, caught up in an unending grief. I grieve for the lives lost that day, most certainly. But I also grieve the life that I lost that day, the life that I had known up till that fateful morning. The person I was on September 10, 2001, no longer exists, and I have struggled to discover who it is I am now.

Even though I had the love and support of my family, I lived in an incessant cycle of mourning. I've been stranded in the middle of a desert for quite a while, dried up spiritually. I can't seem to get a handle on a definition of God or any Higher Power that can change the way I look at my life, which had already been changed the moment my foot hit the pavement of the streets surrounding the World Trade Center the morning of 9/11.

I want to wince when someone suggests that God must have saved me for a reason. I recoil inwardly at that suggestion because there is no reason I should have lived when so many others didn't. And I can't believe in a God that would "pick and choose" among us that horrific morning.

Yet, having survived, I'm burdened with personally wanting this life of mine to count for something. I don't know if there is a God or other Higher Power that can provide me with purpose. I sometimes ask the universe to let me be aware of doors to be opened or paths to be taken. I don't know if that is foolish, but it gives me a reason to at least keep going one day at a time. But do things like opening doors and discovered paths to be taken really happen?

I'm hoping that finding a usefulness in life will counter that which is always with me: sadness. Because, despite the good things and loving people that I have in my life, there is always a sadness that I doubt will ever go away completely.

There is a commercial for one of the many antidepressants on the market, and it shows a variety of people with depression in various social situations. Each person is holding, in one hand, a stick with a piece of round cardboard on the top of it, and on the front piece of this cardboard are two dots for eyes and a smile. The "smiley face." They hold it up in front of them so that is what other people see, completely unaware of what is behind that mask. There are times I feel as if I'm holding my own stick with a fake smile when around people.

I know this all paints a rather bleak picture of life, but I'm here to write about my truth and the truth of other survivors. When you've witnessed or lived through something as devastatingly gruesome as what took place on 9/11, there is a part of your spirit that is permanently damaged.

But people have been just as traumatized from tragedies other than 9/11. And they probably live with their own great sadness. I write this for them as well.

Yet, Finding the Good

But I must find some goodness somewhere, or else I would think the bleakness would slowly drain the life out of me.

I mentioned the shifting and change in my priorities. That is a good thing. With my family now the most important aspect of my life, I've entered a much deeper relationship with my parents. We've grown together into an adult relationship with one another. I've learned more about them and their own lives over the years here in Lancaster. Our relationship is an entirely new dynamic.

Since moving in with my parents, I find the goodness in us being there for one another. Over these past years, as I've had to watch them age, I've also had to go through many a medical issue and several hospitalizations. But I never regret that I must, at times, revolve my life around theirs. I'm glad that I'm here for them. I consider it a gift to be able to care for them in these later years of their lives.

So that is something about my life I'm glad for. And it raises those questions that always seem to come up in my life about coincidence or divine intervention or the universe at work—the timing of my moving here and living near enough to them that I can be with them when they need me. All I know is, as they say in AA, I'm right where I'm supposed to be.

And the other aspect of my life I consider a gift is when I get to speak publicly about my personal story of 9/11. I've been fortunate to be featured in some stories on our local NBC affiliate. The Lancaster newspaper has written a couple of articles about my story.

But those things are fleeting. What is truly important to me is when I can speak to an audience of people, no matter how big or small. Over my time here, I've spoken at churches, to civic organizations, at senior centers, and, most rewardingly, to students, from seventh graders to twelfth graders to college students. And I always find them so receptive and respectful and, when there is time for Q&As, the questions are insightful and intelligent. I've noticed a hunger among students to know about the day that shaped the world they have been growing up in, more than what they might read in a history book. That's why our survival stories are so important.

After the Tenth Anniversary

No longer living in New York City, I find each anniversary of that dreadful day in September is problematic for me. By my choice, I now live in a city where there is no one else who knows what it was like to be in New York that day, let alone what it was like to be in front of the Twin Towers.

The weeks leading up to each anniversary are fraught with a self-imposed strict expectation to honor the day, and the lives lost, in a proper way. There is no Ground Zero to go to here in Lancaster, Pennsylvania. For some of the anniversaries, I have figuratively just held my breath and anxiously waited for the day to come and go. For most of them, the apprehension and depression start weeks before. From the beginning of the tenth year, I was thinking ahead to the tenth anniversary. What could I possibly do that would sufficiently bring the proper remembrance to such a significant day?

Fortunately, I was given opportunities, for which I am so grateful, to publicly remember and recognize both that day and my place in it. For the tenth anniversary, I shared my story through newspaper and television interviews. Radio listeners in both Singapore and Australia heard it in my own words. I was given the honor of having a reporter and photographer from the BBC spend the day with me here in Lancaster; that resulted in my story being on the BBC's website. I spoke to 1,800 high school students and a local Rotary Club. I could bear witness to that day during the three worship services at my church on the day of the anniversary, as well as at a memorial ceremony held in Lancaster.

The attention, though, was somewhat bittersweet. I'm glad that people want to know what it was like to personally live through the terrorist attack. Even after ten years, it is still so important to me to tell my story, by any means. That is why I wrote my play and its book adaptation. I feel it is the least I can do to help ensure that we, as a country, never forget, especially for the generations to come. I also feel that, as a survivor, it is the least I can do. It is what I'm called to do.

The most fulfilling moment this year was speaking to the teenagers who were mere children in 2001, who have vague memories that "something bad" happened that day. They were so respectful and attentive as they listened to me. Teachers told me they had never seen the students that quiet at an assembly. You literally could hear a pin drop. When I finished speaking, they stood and offered their applause, which moved me to tears. As I came down from the stage, some of them came up to thank me, a few with tears in their eyes, all with true sincerity on their faces. I will never forget this one boy, blond, short, and husky, who could barely get the words "thank you" out. He hugged me and just cried. I realized, then, that generation truly wanted to know about the day that was to change their world before they were even old enough to know it.

But then the anniversary is over, and the attention ceases. There are no more questions being asked. No more tributes being held. Life goes on, as it should and must. I, myself, go back to my usual routine. The one difference, perhaps, between most others and myself (and other 9/11 survivors) is that I will still be thinking of 9/11 every day. I expect it will continue this way throughout the rest of my life. I will still have moments when I feel the great sadness from a grief that lingers. The images of that day will still come to mind unexpectedly. The memories remain vivid. I am moving forward with my life, but that doesn't mean I can forget.

We 9/11 survivors are still healing. We were drawn onto a battlefield that day, and so many of us are still rebuilding the lives that were destroyed because of it. There are the families that will always grieve over the loved ones they lost that day, and we should be ever mindful of them. But we survivors also grieve for our lives, as we knew them, that were taken from us that day. Luckily, for most people, they respectfully and consciously will only have to remember 9/11 once a year. For those of us who were there, we remember every day.

My Visit to the 9/11 Memorial

On April 6, 2012, I went back to New York for the second time. And, as with my family trip to revisit Ground Zero, this visit was also connected to 9/11. I was going to see the outdoor 9/11 Memorial. I tried to have no expectations.

I took the train in, as before, but this time with some friends and not family. As soon as we came up from Penn Station, we caught a cab and went straight down to the Memorial. We were left off in front of my old office building, 195 Broadway, and I pointed out to my friends that was where I was when the terrorist attack began that day.

We walked around, not sure where to go to get inside the Memorial, which could be seen from the street. Finally, we found the line for the Memorial at the northwest corner of Albany and Greenwich Streets. We took our place at the end of a very long line.

We each held a pass needed to get in. One can't just go to the Memorial on a whim. You must reserve a free ticket online; print it out and have it with you always, along with a photo ID. I had reserved our tickets weeks before, which would allow us to enter the Memorial at 5:00 p.m.

I was thankful for the pleasant weather, since we were standing outside. But I immediately began to feel uneasy. The line was too reminiscent of being at an airport or waiting to get on a popular ride at an amusement park as the line snaked around, back and forth, in a formation formed by stanchions and ropes. Something about that bothered me.

There were so many people in line, and I knew we were all there to see the Memorial, but I wasn't there out of curiosity or with a sincere desire to see where the tragedy had taken place. I was there in line because I had been on the ground where the Memorial now stood the morning of 9/11. So, for me, this was as if I was waiting to see a loved one laid to rest. It didn't feel right, standing there among people who were in casual conversations, who occasionally laughed or were joking around out of boredom as they waited for the line to move. Though it certainly might not have been true, I felt I was the only one there because I was connected to those who died on 9/11, the men and women whose deaths I witnessed and those I didn't.

I don't mean to give the impression that I presume that my grief is deeper than anyone else's or that my experience of 9/11 makes me special in any way. We all were affected by what happened on 9/11. After all, we each have a story of that day, whether we were there or across the country or across the globe, whether we lost someone or just wept for all those we didn't know.

There are those, though, who were affected personally, be it losing a loved one, having a physical or mental affliction now, dealing with guilt for surviving, or living with images that can't be erased. What we who were there experienced that day is unique to each of us. We may have witnessed the same things, smelled the same smells, heard the same sounds, but what the day did to us, individually, is our own. The imprints of the trauma on our lives or the repercussions or the losses can't be compared or measured. It is different for every person.

All of this was going through my mind as we eventually came to a sidewalk covered by protective overhead scaffolding that led us to a room where we were scanned, taking off our belts and jackets, emptying our pockets of everything, from wallets to cell phones, just another indication of how our world had changed because of 9/11.

Past security, we were led back outside, where we walked a short distance down another walkway. Turning a corner, we saw the Memorial before us. The first thing I noticed was that all the trees were leafless, bare, and skeletal. They weren't the lush green as pictured in an aerial shot of the Memorial that I had seen. The trees had been symmetrically planted on an expanse of concrete, stark and impersonal. Those two words can also describe what I was feeling. There was no emotion. No tears. That bothered me, and I asked myself why I wasn't feeling anything.

We walked to the south pool, the "footprint" of the South Tower. I watched the water cascading over the sides and, again, nothing. I said to one of the friends with me, "I'm not feeling anything."

We walked over to the north pool, past the structure that will be the museum. That, too, seemed stark in its design. This time, I asked the same friend, "Why aren't I feeling any emotion?" He said, "Maybe because nothing is familiar." Yes. That was it exactly. I was disoriented. I could have been standing in the middle of any random memorial. I wanted to point out to my friends who were with me where the steps were that I ran up the morning of 9/11, running to save the people I saw jumping. I couldn't determine where they might have been. Nor was there any indication of where I had stood under the shelter of Building Number 5 as I helplessly watched, unable to rescue anyone.

Yes, the two pools allowed me to know where the Twin Towers stood, but there was nothing that reminded me of all that the World Trade Center had been. The plaza between the North and South Towers had always been vibrant and full of life, especially in the summer. The noontime concerts, the food vendors and their carts, the benches we all sat on as we ate lunch, the fountain in the center of the plaza. There was nothing to convey to people who had never seen the World Trade Center before just how magnificent it was—the "city within a city," as I called it.

The centerpiece of that glorious fountain in the center of the plaza was *The Sphere*, the sculpture created by Fritz Koenig. *The Sphere* had been found amid the rubble and debris after 9/11. It was damaged but still whole. The finding of it was one of those small stories during such a dark time that shone a bit of light, a suggestion of hope. It was then, at that time, on display in Battery Park, but I was wondering why it wasn't here in the Memorial, standing exactly where it once stood. That would have given the Memorial a much-needed familiarity. Ironically, I found out the next day that *The Sphere* was supposedly being moved from Battery Park to be stored in an airport hangar.[1] Though at one time promised that *The Sphere* would be part of the Memorial, it is not going to be. Supposedly, the designers stated it couldn't be there to protect the integrity of the design. I say to hell with the design. *The Sphere* belongs as the focal point of the Memorial. The decision to not let it be and the city's acceptance of that decision were, to me, unconscionable.

Along each of the two pools are the names of all who died on 9/11 etched on the sides. I wanted to find the names of Joe and Judd. There was a paper brochure to help locate individual names. I found each of their names, close together, and ran my fingers along the engraving of their names.

Also, during our time there, I would text Stephanie because she knew this might be difficult for me and said she would be available via text messages if I needed to contact her. I sent her quite a few text messages.

---

[1] *The Sphere* is now located in Liberty Park near the World Trade Center.

We had planned on staying at the Memorial until dusk because I was told it was beautiful at night. I hope it is. But I didn't want to spend any more time there; so, we left.

Upon exiting, we passed a visitors center. I was hoping that the center would have what the Memorial was lacking at this point. I was hoping there might be pictures of the World Trade Center before 9/11. Or, better yet, a miniature model of it. I wanted my friends and other visitors to see for themselves what a wonderful place the World Trade Center had been. But, sadly, there was nothing of the sort. Instead, it was filled with 9/11 Memorial souvenirs. It was a gift shop where one could buy a 9/11 Memorial pencil or T-shirt or coffee mug, or the men's 9/11 Memorial silk tie for $79.50. I finally felt an emotion, and it was anger. This is what the tragedy of 9/11 has been reduced to—a souvenir key chain?

I want to believe that most people who will visit the 9/11 Memorial will do so with the sincerest of motives, to remember that day in September and those who died. But I fear that for some, it will primarily be a tourist attraction, something to add to the list of "what to see while in New York City," along with the Empire State Building and the Statue of Liberty.

I know that I am in the minority in my reaction to the Memorial, particularly among other 9/11 survivors, and I am thankful for that. I truly am glad that the Memorial can be a place of consolation and comfort for others. I'm glad the 9/11 families have the Memorial as a physical tribute to memorialize their loved ones.

But, I will hold on to my memory of kneeling before Ground Zero (that weekend before returning to work), overcome by the holiness of that spot. Sadly, that ground I considered so sacred is now covered with cement slabs and throngs of tourists.

Perhaps nothing built to commemorate that day could be a place of comfort for me.

I hope my sentiment about the Memorial offends no one. If it does, I do apologize. But mine is just one opinion, a singular reaction.

Though I didn't personally know anyone who lost their life on 9/11, I feel personally connected to all those who died. Their deaths affect me to this day. I had never witnessed the death of anyone until that morning. There are images that will be with me for the rest of my life. I want to bring honor to the memories of those who are gone. And I want people who never went to the World Trade Center to know what a magical, extraordinary place it had been, with its buildings, the Twin Towers, the plaza, and the people.

Those of us who were there should never stop telling our stories of that day, remembering the ones who died. The people of New York City who worked there or shopped there or took visiting friends or relatives there can keep memories of the World Trade Center itself alive. And people all over the world will always remember their first impressions of those monumental Twin Towers when seeing them for the first time. We can each be a small piece of a mosaic of recollections, reflections, and remembrances of the World Trade Center.

I am grateful that I'm here today to tell my story, knowing there are so many stories of that day that we will never know. So, I will do what I can to ensure that people never forget.

Perhaps that can be my own personal memorial to 9/11.

On the Eleventh Anniversary of 9/11

I had been watching an HBO series called *The Newsroom*, a show centered on a fictional cable network and its flagship news show. Each episode's fictitious storylines revolve around a factual, significant news story of a specific day in the past few years.

One episode, titled "5/1," featured a plotline that revolved around the major news story of May 1, 2011, the death of Osama bin Laden.

From the perspective of just a TV viewer, it was riveting to watch what it must have been like in newsrooms across the country that day as the story we had all been waiting for had finally become a reality. But as someone who had witnessed, and survived, the 9/11 attack in New York City, it was difficult to watch.

As I watched the *Newsroom* episode, my thoughts quickly went from the night of 5/1/2011 to the morning of 9/11/2001. The images, memories, helplessness, pain, and sorrow of that day when everything changed are always with me. Most of the time, they are just in the recesses of my thoughts, no longer inhibiting me from my daily routines. Yet there is always an underlying anticipation that all those things can rush to the forefront of my thoughts as I relive that day. Sometimes they are triggered by something specific, other times by nothing at all. This time, it was a television show.

And it's not just the images I recall. It is also the emotions still so closely associated with those images, the terror and fear, the feeling of utter helplessness, the anguish, the sorrow.

I became aware that I was biting down on my knuckle while watching the TV, hoping that would prevent the tears falling down my face, breaking into outright sobs. A friend was sitting in another chair, watching with me. If he was aware of what was going on with me, he didn't say anything.

Every 9/11 survivor I've communicated with shares the fact that there are people who think we should be "over it" by now, unable to understand why we haven't "moved on." I think I can say on behalf of many survivors that we will never be "over" it. The memories of 9/11 are with us daily, some days just unobtrusively in the background, some days occupying every conscious thought.

And even though it has been eleven years now, as each anniversary approaches, I am acutely aware of it. I feel on edge, easily irritated by the smallest insignificant things. The memories seem fresher, as if 9/11 had happened only yesterday. I cry more than usual. As if the anniversary of a family member's death is near, the grief over the lost lives of people I didn't even know is no less.

I have made progress in this mourning process. I may not have "moved on," but I am moving forward.

But I will never forget that day in September, back in 2001. And I will do what small part I can in ensuring the generations to come will learn to always remember.

Visiting the 9/11 Museum

It was in May 2014. The week before the 9/11 Memorial Museum was to open to the public, there was a dedication period where those affected directly by 9/11 could walk through the museum with others whose lives had also changed that day. The families who lost a loved one, the first responders, the firefighters and police, the cleanup workers who cleared away all the debris of the fallen towers and the survivors were extended the privilege and the honor of remembering that day and those who died.

I knew that, for me, and probably for all of us, it would also mean reliving that day. But I had to go.

The invitation to visit the museum allowed me to bring a guest. Neither of my parents would be able to make the trip with me because of their health, so there was no question who I wanted to go with me: my therapist, Stephanie. Over the past years, she, more than anyone, has listened to the intimate details of my story of 9/11, the details that I leave out if talking to others about that day. She is the one who sees the tears that I try to keep my parents from seeing. She graciously accepted my invitation.

We took the train to NYC on May 17.

At the museum, there were no lines, no waiting, no tourists. We were ushered into the massive halls of the museum, filled that day with the stillness of sorrow. The only sounds I was aware of, initially, were my own sobs, which were caused by what we first encountered as we began our walk through the memories of 9/11. It was black-and-white photos of people in the streets that morning, staring up at the towers, just as I did. Though my face wasn't in any of the photos, it could have been in any and all of them. The one unmistakably noticeable thread that wove through each of those photos was the faces tilted upward all had the same look—that of shock, disbelief, fear, horror. All the raw emotions that I'm sure were on my face as well that morning as I, too, looked up in total incomprehension. As the photos of faces in the streets faded one into another, there was audio playing of eyewitness accounts. Just one or two sentences from many of those who had been there that morning, describing what they had seen and felt. Descriptive and detailed words that Stephanie later told me she had heard before from me in my numerous sessions with her over the years.

The museum is filled with historical artifacts that I'm sure will elicit emotional responses from future visitors. For me, it was the things that are part of my own story that connected with me, that caused me to continue to cry till I didn't have any tears left nor the physical stamina to allow any to flow. The wall with images of the flyers that had been posted throughout the city in the days that followed 9/11, each with a different face and the word MISSING on them. The room discreetly placed in the museum with photos of the victims often callously referred to as "the jumpers," who will always be courageous heroes to me because they were faced with the decision of how they would die. They are who I think of often—the falling people. Their descents toward death are the images that haunt me the most. I often wonder how many of them had prayed to God that morning they wouldn't die. Prayers that, if heard, were unanswerable.

There are two quotes in this area from eyewitnesses which are on a wall in the 9/11 Museum.

> She had a business suit on, her hair was all askew. This woman stood there for what seemed like minutes, then she held down her skirt and then stepped off the ledge. I thought, how human, how modest, to hold down her skirt before she jumped. I couldn't look anymore.
> —James Gilroy, Lower Manhattan resident

> You felt compelled to watch out of respect to them. They were ending their life without a choice and to turn away from them would have been wrong.
> —Louisa Griffith-Jones, Lower Manhattan resident

Upon turning one corner, we were confronted with walls of photos of every person who died that day. There, in that room, I was overwhelmed by the sheer number of faces that reflected just how unbelievably horrific

9/11 really was. And being one who lived, staring at those who didn't, I was conflicted by the wavering emotional pull of being grateful my face was not on those walls while also partially wishing it was. Does survivor's guilt ever go away?

As our two-hour tour of the museum was ending, we came upon a room that I had so hoped would be there: a room dedicated to what the World Trade Center was pre-9/11. In the center of the room was a large-scale model of the Twin Towers and the massive plaza that connected them and the surrounding buildings that were also part of the World Trade Center. I could finally show Stephanie what I had only been able to describe in our sessions. I pointed out to her my path that morning, where I ran to when I so desperately wanted to reach the North Tower, and where I was when the second plane hit the South Tower. What stood before us was the place I had worked across from and had grown to love, where I would sit with a cup of coffee and the newspaper each morning before going into my office building, the plaza where I spent most lunch hours. The place that was to become, and will always remain to me, "Ground Zero." Sacred ground that I wish had remained untouched.

It has been two weeks and a day since I walked through the 9/11 Memorial Museum. It has been a difficult two weeks. I was affected by the museum more acutely than I had expected. But I'm glad I went. I had to because I was there the morning of September 11, 2001—a date now etched in history books and the memories of those personally affected by the catastrophic tragedy on that date.

The words "never forget" expressed our country's emotional response to the senselessness of 9/11. The 9/11 Memorial Museum will now remind each generation to "always remember."

A 9/11 Survivor's Second Chance for a Life-Changing Day?

I took a sick day from work last week because I was having a COPD (chronic obstructive pulmonary disease) flare-up, when my usual shortness of breath gets worse.

I was diagnosed with COPD about a year ago. It is a progressive disease, which means it will get worse over time. At sixty-three, I was told I have the lungs of an eighty-eight-year-old. The toxins from Ground Zero led to my having this disease, as well as gastroesophageal reflux disease and sleep apnea. All three are listed as 9/11-related illnesses caused by exposure to the air of Ground Zero.

It is very common among 9/11 survivors, first responders, and search-and-rescue teams to develop a variety of illnesses from exposure to the airborne toxins of 9/11, all these years later. I belong to a Facebook group of 9/11 survivors, and frequently, someone will post about his or her newly diagnosed sickness or continuing struggle with PTSD or, sadly, the passing of someone whose death was directly connected to 9/11. A lot of cancer among the first responders and search-and-rescue and cleanup crews is causing too many deaths.

So, physically, I am reminded of 9/11 just about every day, which brings me back to being at home, sick. For two days, I had struggled with breathing and a constant, audible raspy wheezing in my chest.

Fortunately, all my 9/11-related physical, mental, and emotional afflictions are being covered through the WTC Health Program, which provides medical monitoring and treatment to those of us who were exposed to toxins and psychological stressors related to the 9/11 attacks.

I saw the pulmonary specialist the program assigned to my case and was put on a steroid. Little did I know, till after the fact, that my moods and emotions were going to fluctuate wildly. I found this out when I decided to rewatch *Ghost* on Netflix.

Under normal circumstances, I'm sure I would have become emotional during the final minutes of the film. But by the time I was at the last part of the movie, I was far beyond just a few tears.

I started to cry uncontrollably, my thoughts bombarded with memories of the many people during my lifetime that death has taken from me. From my two-year-old brother, when I was five, to my best friend, and others, who died from AIDS, to friends who had taken their own lives, and to relatives long gone. I even projected the eventual passing of my parents.

Most of the memories, though, were vivid images of the people I witnessed falling to their deaths from the Twin Towers on 9/11. I couldn't stop those mental pictures or the tears that accompanied them. Tears I still shed for those complete strangers I have an unexplainable connection to.

When something good happens to someone, it is common for him or her to casually say that "it changed my life." Or if it is something unfortunate or bad that happens, to say "my life hasn't been the same since."

For me, 9/11 was unquestionably and emphatically the day everything changed for me. My life, as I knew it, was gone. Like Humpty-Dumpty, my entire being was shattered, and I am still, fifteen years later, trying to put the pieces back together again. I continue to feel as if I am floundering, some days barely clinging to the determination to just get through the next twenty-four hours.

Since that day when everything changed for me, unexpected happiness has seemed foreign, as has unexpected life changes. This is the definitive standard by which I've lived the past dozen years or more.

But last week, my rigid expectation to expect nothing was confronted with something potentially life changing. My giving up on hope was challenged by something possibly full of hope.

As unforeseen as how my life changed on September 11, 2001, so was an email I received on Thursday, May 26, 2016.

At the beginning of May, I sent an email to Arianna Huffington with a piece I had written about 9/11. I somewhat timidly wrote her, asking if she might consider publishing it on *The Huffington Post* as the year's fifteenth anniversary of 9/11 drew near. My expectations were not high as I considered how many emails she must receive daily, wondering if she even read them herself.

But, last Thursday, a day I don't think will easily be forgotten, I received an email reply from Ms. Huffington herself. It simply stated, "Dear Artie, many thanks for thinking of us and for sending me your post. We would love to feature your voice on HuffPost. I'm cc'ing our blog editor M. W. to send you a password so you can start blogging on the site. All the best, Arianna."

I can't remember the last time I was speechless or felt a rush of pure excitement and joy. I thought myself incapable of ever knowing those feelings again.

I was back at work and read the email to my coworkers, which helped make it real. Their enthusiastic congratulations heightened my elation. And I dared to be happy! A huge achievement for me.

You see, Ms. Huffington's email is more than just welcomed words. It is an email full of significance for me.

People are constantly asking me what I am writing because I proved to myself, and others, that I can write, having written a play, its adaptation into a book, and many blog posts, letters to editors, and articles. I have been told that I am a good writer, and I graciously accept that compliment.

I like to write. I always have. But I never felt I had a reason to until 9/11. And I discovered, or perhaps rediscovered, there is a deep desire to express myself in written words. But often, I come up with excuses not to write. Insecurities. Fear of rejection. The usual things we come up with to stop us from doing what we would really like to be doing.

I am sincerely grateful to Ms. Huffington because she has given me a platform to write and hopefully reach others with my words. Oh, I'm still insecure and fear people might not like what I write, but I can't ignore this advantage that had been offered to me so generously.

There is no longer room for made-up excuses. Maybe what I will write in my blogs won't go beyond just a readership of friends and family, but, for the first time in such a long time, I feel hope. And that perhaps something good might be possible for my life. Life-changing? That may be a stretch. A personal sense of accomplishment? Most certainly, I hope.

Post-Traumatic Stress Disorder and Its Triggers (Orlando)

I attempted to write a blog the previous night, but my thoughts weren't coherent. I was trying to comprehend the magnitude of the horror in Orlando. I knew better, but I made the mistake of exposing myself to too much television and internet coverage.

Since 9/11, whenever a traumatic event happens somewhere, it becomes a trigger for me, bringing up all that I associate with 9/11.

Those living with PTSD must navigate through each day carefully, as if walking on fields filled with hidden land mines. On the best of days, we are somehow able to maneuver through unscathed emotionally, mentally, and psychologically.

But often we inadvertently take a misstep, detonating an explosion. Not of projectiles of weaponry but of images and emotions and memories of sights, smells, and sounds of 9/11.

It's impossible to be vigilant every hour, and we are often lulled into thinking we will be free of any triggers, if even for just a day.

But often we don't need an explosive moment to transport us back to 9/11. Sometimes it's little eruptions.

For me, it's a cacophony of sirens, fire trucks, ambulances, or police cars.

Or a beautiful day, with the sky as blue as it was the morning of 9/11.

It can be depression or anxiety that sneaks up on me.

Or watching a movie filmed in New York pre-9/11, when the Twin Towers were a striking part of the city's skyline.

It can come out of nowhere. This morning, I was driving to Starbucks. My window was down, my sunroof open, and gentle music playing. Serene.

But then I saw, in my mind's eye, a person falling down the length of one of the towers, my serenity suddenly replaced with sadness and grief.

But these triggers are the incidentals of my life now. For all survivors of trauma.

I first saw something on Facebook about Orlando and turned the TV on just at the beginning when there were few facts. I, like many others I'm sure, sat transfixed. In shock, yet still watching.

When the confirmed, hard facts started coming in, that's when I should have turned the TV off.

But the footage was now being shown of the people. Injured, bloody, being carried by others.

The abundance of my 9/11 memories began blending with what I was seeing on TV. Images on television matching my images of 9/11.

One man's story hit me hard. He told of escaping with his buddies by jumping a fence and hiding behind a car. From his place of concealment, he saw a young injured man, who had been shot three times, and he ran to him to take him to safety and to start treating his gunshot wounds.

On 9/11 I was escaping from the impact of the second plane hitting the South Tower, dodging the falling debris. I saw the injured man lying in the street, everyone running past him. But, I stopped and ran back to him.

His injury wasn't a gunshot wound, but a split skull, blood pouring from it.

I know, intellectually, there was only so much I could do on 9/11; but that doesn't bring comfort.

When I first realized there were people jumping from the North Tower, and I started running to them, to get as close as I could get to the North Tower, the falling debris in the plaza stopped me.

There are times I wish I hadn't thought of my own safety and had run to those people anyway. I wish I had been brave enough to be willing to die trying to help. That is another regret I will live with the rest of my life.

I share these hard and difficult truths with you so that you know that no matter how many years go by, those of us who survived 9/11 will always live with triggers.

That is true for the victim of any trauma or tragedy. It is just a fact of our lives.

My heart was so heavy last night, filled with grief and sadness. I sat down to dinner with my folks. Usually, I am talkative, but I was silent. All three of us were. I didn't know if my folks were aware of my quietness or if they thought I was upset at them for some reason.

If they had asked, "What's wrong?" I know I would have just burst into tears. The weight on my heart was too heavy to try to speak. So, I couldn't bring it up.

Even now, I remain detached and silent.

Ironically, tomorrow I must speak to one-hundred-plus men at a luncheon about my experience of 9/11. There's no way to prepare what I'll say. Or if I'll be able to even get words out. I will just have to trust that I'll be open and that I will speak truthfully and unflinchingly.

Our Students Need to Hear Our Stories of 9/11

When my play, *That Day in September,* opened Off-Broadway in 2003, I didn't regard it as a theatrical triumph. I wasn't an actor playing a part in someone else's play. I was simply being myself, sharing my story of 9/11, in my own words. That was triumph enough.

It's not that my story was of great significance. There are thousands of stories from all who survived that horrific morning.

But each time I tell my story, I feel I am accomplishing two things.

First, that it is one way I can honor and pay tribute to all who died that day. And, second, I can contribute in my small way to help ensure that we, as a country, never forget.

That is why I wrote and performed my play. Just to be on a stage telling an audience what I witnessed and survived on 9/11.

Since then, I have spoken to seventh to twelfth graders and college students.

Students will read about 9/11 in history books. But the words on a page pale in comparison to hearing the words of those who were there and survived and have their stories to tell.

It is these stories that will ensure future generations will never forget. 9/11 has become our country's second "date which will live in infamy."

There is a quote attributed to Rudyard Kipling that sums up best how I feel when speaking to students: "If history were taught in the form of stories, it would never be forgotten."

I have a new ambition now, and that is to share my story with as many students as possible. But I'm not finding many open doors. Quite the opposite, unfortunately.

Last autumn, I sent fifty emails to each school district superintendent and the principals of every middle and high school in two local counties, offering to speak. I only heard back from one person: a teacher in an English language arts program. Because of him, I spoke to eighth graders at his middle school this past May.

They were quiet and so very attentive to my story. The teachers commented on the silence as the students listened to me.

I find that even youth at this age have a desire to know all they can about the day that shaped this world they are living in. I will share what I have to say as long as I can.

Orlando. Istanbul. And Memories of 9/11

I can't count how many times I've been asked, "Are you writing?" by well-meaning friends and acquaintances. It is always with a bit of embarrassment to answer with "no."

But each time someone asks me that question, I am deeply touched because it means that my written words must touch people. I've wanted to continue to write for that very reason, but always found an excuse not to put my fingers on my keyboard.

This opportunity to write for *The Huffington Post* allowed me no excuses now.

But, I questioned what I hoped to accomplish.

My focus had been, and probably will continue to be, on being a 9/11 survivor and living with PTSD.

But I must admit that I worried what my readers will think.

"Is this all he can write about?"

"Isn't he over this yet?"

"Why doesn't he just move on with his life?"

These are all questions that survivors of 9/11 assume people are thinking about. And some survivors, who are my friends, have had someone ask them one of those inappropriate questions to their faces.

So, for the most part, we, the survivors of 9/11, remain publicly silent. We feel the need to conceal what we go through daily. We are "in the closet," hiding our individual effects of our PTSD.

So, I've questioned what I should write about, and the answer came in a comment under one of my blogs.

I'm a 9/11 survivor as well. Since I moved to Texas, nobody gets it. So glad my friend told me about you.

B.

So, for now, I'll continue to write what I feel prompted to write about, with thanks to B.

Which brings me to the title of this chapter and the horror we had been witnessing throughout the world during many weeks.

When I first learned of the terrorist attack at the airport in Istanbul, my thoughts went to Orlando and from there to 9/11.

I watched the television and the horrible hectic video of people running for their lives in the airport.

And then I thought of the people who had nowhere to run inside Pulse.

And those of us in the streets surrounding the World Trade Center running helter-skelter, seeking safety from the falling debris of the second plane's impact.

One week was a terribly difficult week for me. I couldn't rid myself of the images of what was shown outside Pulse, in the streets.

And though I know many people probably won't understand this, I imagined being inside Pulse when the carnage started.

Not to be a hero and stop the terrorist. I'll probably have to figure this one out with my therapist.

But I know what it is like to be in a life-and-death situation, where thoughts of possibly dying mix with wanting to help those who are dying. Maybe I imagined being in Pulse because I hope I could have been able to do there what I feel I failed to do on 9/11.

I know logically and intellectually there wasn't anything I really could have done on 9/11 to help others without putting my own life in jeopardy. But still …

I still don't know why, but I was driven by a desperate need to be with those who I watched fall into the plaza. Even knowing they were all dead, I kept thinking what if one person was still barely alive. If so, I wanted to be there to hold his or her hand. I didn't want that person to die alone.

So perhaps that's why I placed myself in Pulse, imagining doing there what I was unable to do as I stood under Building 5's edge in the plaza of the WTC.

I was given the opportunity after the second plane hit to help an unconscious dying man in the street. But still I wish I could have done more.

There is a video on YouTube of Anderson Cooper covering the terrorist attack in Orlando, bravely facing a camera as he says the names of all who died inside Pulse. I tried to watch it a few days ago but had to stop after just a few of the names.

But last night, perhaps prodded by what had taken place in that airport in Istanbul, I watched the video all the way through, and I cried as Anderson cried while doing his best to say each name.

Hearing the names, seeing some of the photos of those who died reminded me of the pieces of paper taped on every conceivable place available in the streets of the city days after 9/11. Each with the word MISSING underneath a photo of someone. Most of the photos showed the missing person in a happy moment. A wedding. A party. With family. Seeing those faces made it so very real. Listening to the names of Orlando did the same.

But there have been so many other bombings and attacks that don't get as much attention, and we never get to hear their names or see any faces.

Perhaps we would all go mad if we were to truly pay attention to every life taken in every act of terrorism.

There is a vast difference between how people react to terrorism. The reactions of those who have survived a terrorist attack and those who are fortunate to have never had to witness such horrors.

Just Do the Next Right Thing

I lost my job of twelve years this past Saturday. I was laid off. Instead of being angry, depressed, or bitter, I'm pleasantly at peace about it.

There's that saying in twelve-step programs: "Just do the next right thing." When I left NYC to move to Pennsylvania (against all sensible logic), I knew it was the next right thing to do. And I've never regretted making the move.

And now it was time to once again do the next right thing. I needed to leave my job. My heart was no longer in it. Nor was I passionate about it, even though it was an enjoyable place to be. I worked with people who were more like friends or family. But sometimes people must finally leave their family and find their own new way in the world.

But how to make such a change? How to do this next right thing?

I went and got tattooed on my back "Just Do the Next Right Thing."

I thought of early retirement, knowing it wasn't the wisest decision. I was in a quandary. So perhaps my being laid off was God or the universe (I'm still not sure about my faith) giving me a gentle nudge toward that next right thing.

I was asking myself the question of what to do with the last quarter of my life. I asked God, the world, and the universe (that faith thing again) what I could bring to the table of life. Could I leave behind an indelible lasting impression?

I assume most of us want to believe we will leave our mark on the world. We want to trust that our lives will have meant something. For some, just being remembered fondly by family and friends will be enough. But for some, we want our life's footprint to reach far beyond our closed little circle of people.

Being a 9/11 survivor has much to do with that. Part of any survivor's remorse or guilt is the question that can never be answered (at least in this lifetime). That question of "Why did I survive when so many others didn't?" Being a single man, I often think why it couldn't have been me, in place of a loving husband, father, wife, or mother.

I sit in Starbucks typing this, my eyes filling with tears. I still grieve for those who died, and when they come to mind, it is as if it was only yesterday that I saw people falling down the length of the towers to hit the ground and have their life taken from them.

I take a break from typing, suppressing the sob that is near the surface, and wipe the tears from my eyes. I compose myself and sip from my iced coffee.

Back to the question of what I wanted to do with the next years of my life. I know what my passion is. To tell my story of 9/11. And of the years since then. And perhaps, one day, of my years before 9/11.

I cherish opportunities to share my story publicly. I am driven to find a way to make more speaking engagements a possibility. With the help of one of my former bosses, I will be looking for an agent or manager who can do the legwork of finding those opportunities to tell my tale.

And I will have a companion by my side. A four-legged companion named Ranger, my new service dog, trained to be with owners who suffer from post-traumatic stress disorder, as I do. I have been wanting a service dog for quite some time now. I was accepted by two local organizations that place service dogs, but there was a one- to two-year wait to even meet a potential match.

Then I got a call from New Hope Assistance Dogs Inc. in Warren, Pennsylvania. The president, Tammy Rogers, said she thought she had a match for me. A match based on her instinct, intuition, and years of experience matching service dogs to their humans.

I drove five hours to Warren, Pennsylvania, two weeks ago and met Ranger. It was love at first sight. At least it was for me. I can't speak for Ranger. But my first night there, Ranger stayed with me at the hotel and lay snuggled up beside me as we slept. At one point, I put my hand on his side and kept it there as my hand went up and down with each breath he took.

I left Warren, knowing I had met my dog. The next step was raising the money for him. I needed to raise seven thousand dollars.

If I ever need to be reminded of the goodness in people, all I must think of is how quickly the money was raised. I received generous donations from friends and from their friends whom I didn't even know (thanks to the Share feature on Facebook). I got donations from New Zealand, Germany, and someone in England I don't even know. The complete sum has been raised, and I hope by next week, Ranger will be by my side.

Two months ago, I was filled with sadness and despair. I'm sure both of those emotions are just around the corner, ready to pounce out at any given moment, but now I won't fight the battles alone. I'll have Ranger by my side. And my parents, who have been a constant source of support.

A month ago, it was as if I had these giant puzzle pieces on a table in front of me and I wasn't sure how to piece them together. But I figured it out and the puzzle is completed.

My 9/11 Blog

On this anniversary of 9/11, I know I must write something. But what I want to write is going to be less somber than one might expect from a survivor who still lives with the pain and burden of unrelenting sadness daily.

The tone will be lighter because among the emotions that accompany my grief, survivor's guilt, and unhappiness is a buoyancy brought to me by a four-legged new companion, Ranger, my PTSD service dog, who I just brought home this past Sunday. And now exactly a week later, the bonding between us is undeniable. I did spend a previous weekend with him, when we first met. That weekend was to see if we would seem like a good match. With much thanks to New Hope Assistance Dogs Inc., they saw the potential for a possible lifelong relationship.

I grew up with our family seeming to always have a dog, but, as an adult, I never owned a pet. So, I had the hesitations, reservations, fears, and uncertainty that I assume a man would have when he finds out he's going to be a father.

But I also had the excitement, hopes, wonderment, and certainty that I would give it my all and that I believed in my new favorite saying, "Just do the next right thing."

Getting Ranger seems like the next right thing for me in my life. I'm beginning my third week of unemployment, and money will become scarce, but there's another saying I like, which is "More will be revealed."

I know that won't ensure I'll be financially solvent, but I'm back to that basic of one day at a time.

What has Ranger brought into my life in this very short period of time? Love, to put it simply. Now, I love my parents, other family members, and dear friends, but this type of love is where I have the obligation (accepted without reservation) to show each day this four-legged new friend of mine that I am here for him … every day.

And I will express that love in promising him protection, nourishment, and commitment. And, in return, I already know he will look to me as his provider of the above. In this short period of time with him, I know already what people mean when they talk about the unconditional love of an animal. I was going to write "love of a pet," but Ranger is more than a pet. He is promising his protection over the horrors of 9/11 that are always just a thought or memory away.

He will nourish me with his devotion and distraction from the grief and sadness that are still with me daily. And he will commit to be there when I just need to pet him or take his face between my hands and look into his beautiful coffee-colored soulful eyes and tell him I love him and that he is the best dog in the world.

I am getting through this year's anniversary as I usually do: by sharing my story of 9/11 publicly with others. I spoke at a high school and received an email written by a student. She wrote, in part,

> Your presentation was unlike anything I have ever read, heard, or seen about 9/11. From your story, I got a deeper sense of what the event was really like and it helped me better understand the tragedy. ... Your presentation was incredibly informative and insightful and helped the students of Manheim Township and I better understand the event that changed America forever. Thank you so much for taking the time out of your day to come and speak at our high school, we all appreciate it very much.

It is words like that which help me get through this horribly rough period. So, what have I learned in this short time with Ranger? I have not "moved on." I still think about 9/11 every day. I still have flashbacks and replay the "what if" scenarios again and again. I can be moody and irritable and full of anxiety and take it out on those I love. I'm still forgetful and find it very hard to concentrate on any one thing. I still cry. Weep. Sob. I grieve still for the lives lost. I still wish, at times, I had been among them.

Sadness and despair are always on standby, ready to intrude on my day at any time. I still wish 9/11 had never happened. So, what have I learned from Ranger? That even when in the deepest despair, we can allow glimmers and moments of hope, joy, and love into our life.

Thanks, Ranger.

Ranger and a Church Dinner

I went to a church dinner one night at a church I didn't even attend on Sundays. There was a big turnout of people, the majority probably members of the church. Long tables were set up, and I sat at the end of one (so Ranger would be out of the way). I was sitting there alone. My reaction was one of mixed emotions. On one hand, I was content with sitting by myself because I wouldn't have to make small talk. On the other hand, I longed for someone to come up and ask if this was my first time there and offer to sit with me.

The reason I was there to begin with was because the day before, at a craft store, I was buying yarn and knitting needles, thinking I could teach myself to knit through YouTube. I thought it could be a good hobby to occupy my mind (and as I wrote those words, I realized it could also be a hobby of isolation).

A woman behind me in line to pay asked me about Ranger (many people do). In explaining why I had him and my idea of trying to teach myself to knit, she told me about that church serving dinner on Wednesdays, followed by small groups, one being a knitting group. So, I decided to leave my comfort zone of staying home and venture out. It was a decision to be more social.

After eating alone, I went to the knitting group. On Ranger's service vest that he wears when we are out in public, it says, aside from "PTSD service dog" and "Do not pet," the words "My owner is a 9/11 survivor." So, of course, that led to me answering some questions (which I don't mind at all). But then one lady, who spoke with a heavy Spanish accent, said, "You must be very happy you lived." I was honest and told her, "Not really." I tried to explain that it is difficult to revel in being alive when so many didn't live.

Her well-intentioned reply was that God had saved me to do something special. I cringe when anyone suggests that God saved me, because that infers He chose not to save another. And the sentiment that I'm alive to do something special seems a nice fairy tale. The reality of my life is I'm an unemployed, laid-off man with a dream of sharing my 9/11 story as much as possible. If God closes a window (losing my job) to open a door, I'm waiting for it to open, and I feel I'm running out of air.

So, I'm angry.

Angry that 9/11 happened. Angry that I'm physically sick and emotionally and psychologically wounded because of 9/11. Angry I left the city I loved, leaving behind the friends I loved. Angry that most days I put on an "I'm fine" mask to wear throughout the day.

I've not written this to solicit any sympathy. I just want to be honest and hope my honesty might help another 9/11 survivor or anyone in crisis. There are things in my life I'm glad about.

I'm glad I'm with my parents, even if it meant leaving New York. I'm glad I have a therapist who has helped me tremendously. Glad my financial needs for 9/11-related medical expenses are paid for by the WTC Health Program. Glad I finally have a service dog.

And glad I've realized knitting isn't for me. Maybe crocheting.

Others' Stories

When the public thinks of 9/11 (particularly as each anniversary approaches), their thoughts turn, first, to those who died. And that is how it should be.

There are the families who lost a loved one. And those lost loved ones also had friends who are left still hurting and grieving.

There are those who were in public service. The firefighters, the police, the EMS workers, all of whom gave their lives in the line of duty, doing what they had been trained for.

It will never be my intention to diminish those deaths. They are who the two words "never forget" are meant for. Their names will be read aloud on September 11, as they are on every anniversary of 9/11. They will be remembered.

And there are the thousands of eyewitnesses of what took place the morning of 9/11. The ones who stood in the streets, transfixed, unable to look away as our minds tried to comprehend what our eyes were seeing.

Some of us, like myself, are still in therapy, grappling with finding our place in this world now that the life we had, or once lived, is gone. Some grapple with their inner demons alone, talking to no one.

We are now spread all over the globe, so many of us, like myself, having moved away from New York City.

Many of us are connected through support groups. I belong to a Facebook group of survivors. Only another survivor can truly understand the other survivors. The loneliness. The constant sadness. The mental anguish. The silent cries for help.

We are more than friends. We are united with one another. I have been helped by people I've never even met face to face. Our relationships of support are built on emails, private Facebook messages, and occasional phone calls.

If you can, think about us on the next anniversary. As you mourn the physical deaths of the innocents, remember the spiritual, mental, and emotional deaths of the survivors.

Those who died take precedence, without question.

I asked some other survivors to share their thoughts, feelings, or stories. I want you to hear from them, not me. You've read enough about me. Now it's their turn.

From Robert Burdick

Crying. Just selected my Facebook cover photo for 9/11 this year. Moisture in my eyes. All the time working at Ground Zero too busy, remembering the living, finding the dead. Hugging a distraught iron worker at Broad and Beaver. Trying to help a Transit Detective with telling his sister her firefighter husband is gone.

Moisture in my eyes. Couldn't bear to go back on the 11th for a few years. Was in the habit of celebrating my birthday, the 10th, in the City, had to leave before the 11th.

Moisture in my eyes. The last firefighter funeral in the Bronx, almost a year later. Standing in the sea of blue. Moisture in my eyes. Finally, on the 11th, standing by the fence at Ten House trying to cry and let it out. In uniform as must be done, Battalion Chief manning the corner makes his way over and says, "Thank you".

Moisture in my eyes. The same corner, the 11th, after 2 Brothers lost in the damn Deutsche Bank building, saying a prayer. Moisture in my eyes. Typed RIP so many times want to tear those keys off my device.

Moisture in my eyes. 15 years later, still see the piles. Moisture in my eyes. Someday the tears will come. Either in a torrent of relief or in joy if I'm worthy to be with the Brothers in Heaven.

From Anne Samachson

Artie, thank you for giving voice to what so many of us feel. After hearing countless times that I should just get over it, forget about it, and move on, I learned to *never* talk about 9/11 with strangers. It is only now, with the help I'm getting through the WTC Health Program, that I'm learning to "come out of the closet" about my experiences.

From Robin D'Zmura

Hi, Artie. I have thought about it and I believe my contribution might be somewhat bland or boring, and maybe not so interesting to your readers. But it is my story of 9/11 and means a lot to me so I'll still tell you a little about the experience. I regard it as happanstance.

I live in rural Western Loudoun County, Virginia, in a hollow off the beaten path. The morning of the attacks I was watching the news coverage on TV as the attacks were occurring. I had already received many calls from friends asking if they could come out to my house because they thought they would be safer out here in the country away from the cities, particularly D.C., Silver Spring, and other cities near our nation's capital.

I understood how they felt not knowing what kind of attack we were under. I had heard, myself, planes were circling my area, so I was actually freaking out. Nobody knew what was happening. I looked out my window and saw a caravan of cars pulling up in my driveway. Some cars I recognized, which were friends who later went to hotels. But there were two cars that weren't familiar.

A family of Hispanic women and young children poured out of the two cars and slowly walked up to my door. I met them outside and, in broken English, they asked me if they could come in and be safe. Among them was an elderly lady in a nightgown, who had just been released from the hospital after open heart surgery. I opened my house to them, of course, but I was still uncertain what was going on.

So, here I was with 12 strangers filling up my house in complete confusion. I had no food in my refrigerator and I was having a panic attack, just wanting to get back to the TV. I wanted to call Andy (my husband) at work, but there were so many people milling around in the house and I didn't know what to do.

Anyway, this went on and on for two days. The family kept asking me to turn off the TV because it would upset the children. I ran out to the grocery store to buy food to feed all the people. One mother had left her little boy's inhaler at home, so this added to the confusion. After they had been settled in I found out that they were also fleeing an abusive husband.

We had a sleepover on the floor. All of this happened during the exact time I was going through my PTSD after a traumatic event of my own. There is so much to tell. This is just the tip of the iceberg. But, if anything, I wanted to share it with you. But there really is so much more. I really bonded with this family.

We each have our stories of that day when everything changed.

The Eyes of a 9/11 Survivor

Consider the eyes of a 9/11 survivor.

If you could look into them intensely, you would see a story in that pair of eyes staring back at you. A story of survival. For some survivors, it's a story that needs to be told again and again, while for others, it's a story they pray they could forget.

If eyes are indeed the windows to our soul, a survivor's eyes will reflect a soul that is tormented. A soul that is in pain. A soul that suffers. A soul that saw too much.

If somehow you could get behind those eyes, and into the memories those eyes hold, you would finally know, perhaps more than you wish, what those eyes witnessed the morning of September 11, 2001.

What I, and every other 9/11 survivor I know, saw that morning could drive a person away from sanity. And for some of us, we teeter on the edge of madness, always fearful of what might push us over the edge. Could it be a familiar sound or smell that brings up a suppressed recollection from the morning of 9/11? Might it be an airplane overhead or the wail of a siren? The screams of children at play? Or perhaps a memory that is too miniscule, or too enormous, to finally face?

We survivors witnessed the horrors of what trained men and women of the military see every day of their active duty. But we had no training for combat. We never expected to find ourselves on a battlefield. Yet that morning, we were reluctantly there on the front lines, standing transfixed by the, up until then, unimaginable.

I received the following email one day from a friend, and I think it applies to all 9/11 survivors. So, I share it with you, as if it were written directly to you.

I just read your latest Huffington Post blog and was silently reflecting for some minutes afterward.

You expressed the same thoughts and emotions that I've heard from so many combat vets in the Team River Runner program (a kayaking group of vets with PTSD).

As I pondered this, I came to the realization that, in fact, you are one of the earliest combat veterans from the continuing global war on terror. This is not allegory. This is truth.

You are as much a veteran as the men who endured the bombardment of Ft. Sumpter, the people who ran from the bombs at Pearl Harbor, and those who stood waiting as the helicopters flew to the roof of the US Embassy in Saigon.

You are a member of this brotherhood. You are not alone … no matter how you feel.

Bill Butler

I still stumble over words to describe what my eyes saw. *Horrific* is the one word that always comes to mind, yet that is a feeble attempt at describing the indescribable.

What I, and the others, saw through our souls' windows stays with us to this day. We never know when a specific image might be projected onto our thoughts as if on an IMAX screen.

And at night, with our eyes closed during a sound sleep, a dream can intrude, and it will be as if heavy, dark draperies that were closed to block out the sun are suddenly thrown open, and instead of the sun pouring in and blinding us, we see a falling body. That is but one of the permanent photographs our eyes took that morning.

You've seen the many photos that were taken that day. You have seen some of what I'm referring to. But you are looking at those photos from a safe distance. For you, they are just photographic evidence of history.

Imagine, if you can, putting yourself in one of those photos. Imagine you are among the onlookers. One of those people who stood transfixed by the catastrophic moments.

Face to Face: Finally Meeting Another 9/11 Survivor

It might seem hard to believe, but in the fifteen years since 9/11, I'd never sat face to face with another survivor. I am friends with other survivors, but I've never met them. We are all in a Facebook group of 9/11 survivors. I've talked on the phone with some of them, have emailed and private messaged with others on Facebook, and I post on the group page regularly.

I have found support and encouragement with these friends I've yet to meet personally. But, I've always longed to meet another 9/11 survivor in the flesh. I've imagined many times what it would be like to talk with someone who would "get me" and easily understand whatever I needed to share. And I would have the same understanding, and identify with whatever he or she had to talk about.

I finally got the opportunity that has been fifteen years in the waiting. I met, in person, another survivor—a gentleman in his fifties. I can't remember how we connected. My short-term memory seems to be getting worse (as is his, coincidentally). I think he contacted me from reading something about me. But that's beside the point. The important factor is we met. At a Bob Evans for breakfast.

For me, once we met at the entrance, shook hands in introducing ourselves, and were sitting at a table, I felt I had just been handed a gift that I'd always wanted.

This courageous man survived both attacks on the World Trade Center, the bombing in 1993 and then that day in September: 9/11. He'll probably question my use of the word *courageous* in describing him because we often see ourselves differently than the people around us do. And, sometimes our personal view of ourselves isn't the most positive. But I saw courage in this fellow survivor because despite living through two attacks, and even though his struggles are strong, he is getting through each day. One day at a time, borrowing from the twelve-step programs.

The daily burden of memories, images, grief, and guilt is something most survivors experience. The fact that this gentleman went through each day with this burden times two is something I can't identify with. But as for 9/11, there is much similarity in what our lives have been like since that day.

In the many things we talked about, our words and sentences could have been interchangeable. Most of what I expressed, he could have expressed, and vice versa.

It was like looking in a mirror. A mirror that reveals all the emotions connected to all the memories and images of 9/11.

I don't mean to suggest that our time spent together was one big "feeling sorry for ourselves" fest. Or that it was all morose and gloom. On the contrary. I can only speak for myself, but it was a genuinely gratifying meeting of two strangers who instantly have become two comrades because of a shared moment in time and history.

"Losing My Religion"

That's me in the corner
That's me in the spotlight
Losing my religion.
—Bill Berry, Peter Buck, Mike Mills, and Michael Stipe

My battle with PTSD didn't really begin in full force until I left New York for Pennsylvania and my folks who lived there, in 2003.

PTSD has caused me to rethink and challenge so many things in my life, faith and God or that Higher Power being among the lot.

What has challenged my faith is 9/11. I can't stop thinking of the people who were trapped on the upper floors of the towers. How many of them prayed for God to save them and not let them die?

But there was nothing God could do. God, if He or She exists, set up the laws of how the universe would work. And being able to miraculously pick each of those doomed people up and place them on solid ground wasn't a possibility. So, God, by His or Her own design, has made Him- or Herself powerless in some instances. If God was unable to answer those pleading prayers of the doomed, then why pray? Is prayer even a viable action?

There was a time my mother was very ill in the hospital and I was driving to the hospital, tears streaming down my face and praying to God not to let her die. But in an instant, it was as if I came up against a brick wall. What if this was her time to leave this world? What if there really was nothing doctors could do? My prayers were useless, merely selfish words being said out loud.

So, I write all of this to try to give you a glimpse as to why I am so uncertain of the existence of God or a Higher Power.

I've written before that on 9/11 my life was shattered, and I am still trying to put the pieces of my life back together again. The piece that contains faith and belief in something other than myself is the one piece I've yet to find. And I fear that piece may have been fractured itself, becoming crushed glass, scattered away by the winds of doubt.

I Need to Be Angry!

I need to be angry right now, so I hope you will indulge me as I vent.

This morning, I had my yearly medical checkup, provided by the WTC Health Program of which I am a participant. I had blood work, gave a urine specimen, and had an EKG, a chest x-ray, and a breathing test. The breathing test was the most crucial because of my COPD, which, probably, is a result of the air I breathed in on 9/11 and during the three weeks I was back at work, breathing in the toxic fumes from the still-smoldering, burning Ground Zero across from my office building.

The breathing test showed that, at the age of sixty-four, I have the lungs of an eighty-eight-year-old. The likelihood of eventually having to be on oxygen is a reasonable assumption. I can't walk from the far end of the parking lot of the local mall without becoming winded. I had to get a handicapped placard for handicap parking.

Add to that the sleep apnea and gastroesophageal reflux disease I live with, both of which are also connected to the air quality of 9/11 and of Ground Zero.

And then there is the PTSD that I live with every day, always reminded of it with moments of uncontrollable anxiety, irritability, tension, and hypervigilance, which is just fear plain and simple. Fearing something bad will happen. Fearing the unknown or uncertainty of people, places, or things. Isolating myself.

And with PTSD comes the memories, flashbacks, and replayed moments of 9/11, asking the "what ifs" and the "could haves" and the "should haves," having to admit the probable reality that there was no other way that morning could have played out, nor my part in it. The helplessness I felt that morning in not being able to do more is probably what saved my life. Yet I still confuse that helplessness as being inadequate and a failure.

I woke from a nightmare last night, crying. And though the nightmare wasn't about 9/11 specifically (my dreams seldom are), it was about death, dying, and feeling helpless.

Ranger, my service dog, was there beside me in bed and woke up, but we've only been together a little over a month, and we're still working out how to "read" each other. It might involve more training, me finding the command words to let him know I need his comfort and his senses tuned in to the clues my body and mood give when in emotional or psychological distress.

Ranger and Joy

My last speaking engagement, in honor of the fifteenth anniversary of 9/11, was in October. I had Ranger, my trusty service dog, with me, as is always the case when I leave the house. Toward the end of the Q&A, I was asked by one of the attendees what differences Ranger has made in my life.

Without hesitation, I said that he brought me joy. I found myself choking up with emotion as I continued, "I had forgotten what it was like to feel that emotion." I can only assume that a certain kind of joy is a gift dogs give to each of their owners, not just those of us suffering under the aftereffects of trauma. But after years of going through life weighted down by all the "bad stuff" in my head, it is nice to feel something other than just sad, even if it's just those special moments I have with Ranger.

Ranger's companionship is something to be thankful for. Even though I live with my parents, I can still tend to isolate in the confines of my room. Ranger, faithfully there by me (even if he's asleep and snoring), takes away my being alone. When he's awake, I find myself having a one-sided conversation with him, choosing to believe he understands, if not the words, then perhaps the unexpressed emotions behind the words.

Comfort is a great delight, exceptionally good and satisfying. It can be a source of pleasure caused by something (or someone) greatly valued or appreciated. I feel all of this toward Ranger, caught up in the bliss of now, of our present together.

But one of the effects of PTSD is that, for a survivor, thoughts of the future are full of uncertainty and the fear of impending unexpected tragedy. One day, as I lay with Ranger on my bed, the contentment I was experiencing was quickly cut short when I realized I have opened my heart and fallen in love with this four-legged creature, who will be loyal and love unconditionally. That is, until that day comes when he'll no longer be here to lie beside me. Or for me to pet. Or snuggle up to. Because he will die. Maybe that came to mind because my niece had recently had to have her ten-year-old Lab given his lasting rest. Or maybe it's because 9/11 survivors tend to focus on loss because we witnessed the deaths of so many.

I am still taken over by the pleasure of Ranger's company. But it's tempered now, knowing there is a dark cloud out there in the future that I will be forced to stand under.

So, all the good I feel from Ranger has its boundaries.

As quickly as it can be given, it can be taken away. And there are some areas of one's life comfort can't reach. And as quickly as it is given, it can be taken away.

And comfort is rarely everlasting. Perhaps I believe this because that's just my resignation to my post-9/11 view of life.

And I know there are other 9/11 survivors who know what I'm writing about.

But my words are not just for those who were traumatized by 9/11. I would believe there are countless others who have had to endure their own "9/11." Those who have lost loved ones. Those who were the sole survivor of a horrible accident. Those who have been abused sexually, physically, verbally, emotionally, or psychologically. I know there are other life experiences I've not mentioned that can be traumatic to an individual. No one is immune from tragedy.

And no one should bear the weight of trauma alone. That's who I write this for.

It has taken me years to finally allow myself to experience comfort and contentment and to speak and write about it. But the shining brightness of it is limited in its reach. Like a lantern in a densely dark forest, the light of comfort can only reach out so far.

Beyond the light of my newly formed comfort, there is still plenty of blackness, comprised of my trauma of being an eyewitness to, and a survivor of, 9/11.

One of Ranger's attributes as a trained PTSD service dog is to bring comfort to me. When he and I lie on my bed to nap, I'm on my left side, his back is pressed up against me, and I put my right arm around his middle and we drift off to sleep, as I feel the moving of his chest as he breathes. That is perhaps my favorite moment because I feel totally safe.

And when I have a flashback or start to feel anxious, I have him to come to me. His eyes are the color of coffee and somewhat droopy. When I look in those eyes, sometimes they seem full of sadness, as if they are reflecting to me what he senses within me.

So, the lesson, if there is one, is it's okay to allow our wounded souls to feel comfort or contentment and sometimes joy, if even for a few minutes. Or, if we're lucky ... a whole day.

This Is How It Is

On the deepest, darkest of days, I've lain in bed at night overcome by the pain, grief, and sorrow of this, my post-9/11 life, and I've prayed to the God, whose existence I question, to let that night be the night I die. I ask because I would be incapable of causing my own death. I've been on the receiving end of someone ending their life twice in my lifetime, so no matter how great my sadness might be, I couldn't leave those who love me with the heartbreak and trauma that would be with them forever.

So, I will lie there also envisioning how my life would have ended on 9/11 if I had attempted to run across the plaza toward the North Tower, as I wanted to. I know I would have probably been hit by one of the pieces of falling debris or one of the men or women who also were falling that morning.

I then turn my thoughts of being too close to either of the crumbling towers when they fell and being crushed beneath the steel and concrete.

I don't share these thoughts to shock or to evoke disturbing concerns or sympathy. I just want to lay open what many, if not most, 9/11 survivors go through, the symptoms of the guilt that comes from having walked away with our physical lives.

Revealing this mental angst is incredibly hard, leaving me feeling publicly exposed and vulnerable. But I hope that, aside from other 9/11 survivors, there will be people who have survived their own traumatic event who will identify with having their life, as they knew it, changed in a moment. And know that the journey of learning to live their changed life will be difficult but achievable.

I feel dead inside most days, empty and incapable of experiencing the life around me. I spend most of my days feigning the range of human emotions one is supposed to feel during any given day.

I honestly don't know if my life will ever be completely joyful again because the memories and images and emotions and regrets of 9/11 are with me every day.

There are those who would say to me, "It was fifteen years ago; shouldn't you be over this by now?" "Be grateful you survived." "Don't you think it's time you moved on?"

If you were there the morning of 9/11, you wouldn't be asking those questions.

This morning, at a Starbucks, I spoke to a friend about writing this. She asked me a question no one has ever asked. "When are you going to forgive yourself for surviving?"

Only now am I realizing how far-reaching her question is.

My life is not completely morose. I have moments, hours, or sometimes a whole day when I get to experience the closest comparison to participating in life that I possibly can.

I will say that having my service dog, Ranger, has made a significant difference in my life, particularly on those days or nights of despair. Though it's not human contact, my dog is the embodiment of unconditional love and acceptance; and that brings me peace, joy, and smiles.

I'm sixty-four, so I have had several experiences that have altered the course of my life journey. Moving to New York. Struggling with accepting my sexuality. Finding a faith I could believe in. Losing that faith. Falling into the whirlpool of addiction. Pulling myself out of it and embracing sobriety.

But, as you might imagine, none of those carried the same weight as witnessing the devastation caused by the terrorist attacks on 9/11.

My life is now defined as pre- and post-9/11, because on 9/11 I was thrust onto a battlefield, and in that moment, my world was one of indefinable, calamitous causalities and unspeakable images. And now I live with the inner wounds that are slow to heal and scars that still are psychologically hidden.

When the Holidays Are
Anything but Happy

If I could have it my way, there would be no December and no Christmas. Since that's an impossibility, I would love to just seclude myself into a cozy cottage until December has passed and Christmas is over. I could see myself taking up temporary residence there the week before Thanksgiving because that's when this whole holiday season begins—a time of the year that I don't enjoy anymore. Not like I used to. Not for some time now. Not since 9/11.

I know I'm not the only one who feels and thinks this way. Most survivors find November and December difficult, second only to September. And this is to remind them that we all have our own reactions and feelings during this time of year and they are all valid, no matter if they are understood by others or not. They are authentically ours.

But, first I want to recognize and address the many people who aren't associated with 9/11, but who struggle through the holiday season as well. It can be one of the most challenging times of the year—whatever the reasons. Feeling lonely, missing someone, or being reminded of someone no longer in your life or on this earth. Feeling hopeless or dangerously close to the end of your rope, hanging on to life by a thread.

I want to acknowledge those who are hurting. The ones who just hope to find the strength to make it through to January 1.

Not everyone wants to participate in the Thanksgiving dinner, the holiday parties, the Festival of Lights, the dreidel and the eating of fried foods, the Christmas Eve service, or Christmas Day itself. And the endless soundtrack of Christmas songs that cruelly give the impression that if you can just make it home for the holidays, everything will be warm and cozy. That concept completely ignores that, for some, being "home for the holidays" can be as unhealthy as hell.

The holidays can be the loneliest time of the year for those who won't be surrounded by family or friends. Some who might be estranged from their family or have no living relatives left. And there are those without friends who think of extending an open invitation to include them.

And my heart breaks for those who must face the holidays for the first time without the family member or friend who died this past year.

The holidays are unfortunately on that dreaded list of "firsts" people must face when they've lost a loved one. There is no avoiding that first Thanksgiving, first Hanukkah, or first Christmas. They must be faced, and it can take all the strength a person can muster to get through those days.

Even if several years have gone by since the death of someone, that doesn't mean it ever gets easier. The absence of that person will always be felt at certain times of the year. The holidays are one of those times.

To the survivors of 9/11 and other tragedies or trauma.

This is directed to those who would think, or have the nerve to say to you, "Don't you think enough time has gone by?" No, not for the families that lost someone. Or the survivors who lost coworkers or friends that horrible morning.

But then there are the thousands of us survivors who didn't lose someone but did lose the normality of our lives. The holiday season is difficult for us as well.

I'm reluctant to even bring up the challenge we survivors face during the holidays because I know some of the statements that people who don't understand would say.

"At least you're here to enjoy your family and the holidays."

"You didn't know anyone who died that day."

"You're going to bring everyone else down."

But I must remind myself and the other survivors of the similarities we share in so many ways, the difficulty of the holidays being one of them.

Every year, as November begins, so does my anxiety, because of the approaching holidays.

I can't help but think of all those who died on 9/11, some whose deaths I witnessed.

I still deal with survivor's guilt or remorse that I'm here and alive and able to be with family. There is a sorrow in my heart that prevents me from being able to be attentive and "in the moment" as the turkey is carved, or gifts are unwrapped, or carols are sung.

The hardest thing to even attempt to convey to people is that, as 9/11 survivors, we deal daily with the loss of the people we were before the first tower was hit. We now view all of life differently, including the holiday season.

The trauma of what we witnessed devastated us, shattering our lives. Like myself, survivors are still trying to put the broken shards of who we once were back together, including that part that enjoyed the holidays. So, we stay silent for the most part on those days.

We might go to the office party or take part in lighting the menorah, or the hanging of the ornaments and tinsel. And we'll listen to the prayers of Thanksgiving recited at church, the synagogue, or the dinner table and not feel an ounce of anything to be thankful for. There is sadness in place of joy. Anxiety instead of good cheer.

If you know someone who is a survivor of 9/11, know we will put on a happy face and go through the motions of each family's traditions. We may appear a little distant or distracted, but please try to remember that we're doing our best.

A 9/11 Survivor Looks into a Mirror

You look at yourself in a mirror, something you might do at least a few times during your day. But this time, it's not just to catch a fleeting casual glance of your reflection.

You want to gaze at your face intently to acknowledge that the face looking back at you is that of a 9/11 survivor. This is the face you want to scrutinize, as if for the first time.

Your face has changed during the past fifteen years. You've aged, maybe a little, maybe quite a bit. If you are past the half-century mark of your life, there may be more gray hair (or less hair) than there was in 2001, a few extra lines along your forehead or at the corners of your eyes or mouth.

If you were in your twenties or thirties on September 11, 2001, there may not be significant visual differences in the face staring back at you.

Whatever your age, you'll notice that you've either gained or lost weight just by the fullness or thinness of your face's shape.

You consider each of your facial features, beginning with your eyes. You concentrate on them, wanting to see beyond just their color. You want to examine them closely with an intense purpose. We're told that our eyes are the windows of our souls, and that is what you genuinely want to uncover: your soul. But you are afraid to look too intently for fear you'll see just how damaged your soul became on September 11, 2001, and how irreversible that damage is.

Your eyes can also reflect the broken spirit of who you once were. That brokenness is an open wound, which resulted from your world being so violently shaken that morning.

You look for a light or twinkle of life within your eyes only to realize they seem to be more dead than alive. Those eyes of yours were the eyes of a civilian the morning of 9/11. That is until you found yourself on a battlefield between the two towers. You were on the front lines and are one of the first veterans of a war that was just beginning.

Your eyes witnessed moments you are still unable to speak about. You saw death, among the destruction, all around you.

You might try looking even deeper into your eyes, hoping to get past the barrier that you mentally placed around some of your memories of that day, protecting yourself with a self-imposed amnesia.

Some memories are best left unreachable, yet you want to fill in those missing moments you can't recall. You want to believe you are brave and strong enough to remember the gaps in your memory of that day because you're afraid you are forgetting something important. Yet, you are also afraid you'll remember something so horrific that it might drive you mad.

You look at your mouth and vaguely recall screaming loudly. Were you screaming out of fear that you would lose your life? Or screaming for someone to come help either you or an injured person you were attempting to aid? Or screaming as you witnessed others' deaths? You might have had your fist in, or your hand over, your mouth, unable to utter a scream or any sound.

Did any words come out of your mouth? Any sentences?

"Oh, dear God, no!"

"What's happening?"

Did you swear or pray, or do a bit of both?

Can you evoke the taste in your mouth that morning? Of the ash, soot, dirt, and God knows what else that filled the air all around you? Looking at your nose, you wonder how much of all that you breathed in that day. What, exactly, settled in your lungs?

Are you reminded of any of the smells? Certainly, the smoke. Perhaps the vapors of fuel. Did death have a smell?

You almost forget to acknowledge your ears. Through them, you took in all the sounds of that morning. The cacophony that still plays in your head. Sirens, shouts and screams, explosions, and the smashing of falling debris. You now know what chaos sounds like.

All the above comes from simply staring at yourself in the mirror. Acknowledging that you are looking at a 9/11 survivor. But before you step away, take one last look and leave off one descriptive word.

As you stare at your face now, know, with certainty, that what you see in the mirror is a survivor.

Nice, France, And One Thousand High School Students

There was a week I had been thinking of what to write about for my latest blog for *The HuffPost*, having a variety of ideas floating around in my head.

But then the tragedy in Nice happened.

Another traumatic event added to a list that is rapidly becoming much too long.

I don't really know what can be written or said that hasn't already been voiced. All I can do is add my own words to the responses being made from around the globe.

For my own mental safety, I refrained from reading too much about this latest attack. I do, however, watch the NBC evening news every night at 6:30 with my dad, so I wasn't completely isolated from the story or images.

All it took was a single camera shot of a child's flip-flop in the street and all my triggers of 9/11 were ignited.

The importance of knowing why it happened seems irrelevant right now compared to the death and carnage that resulted from it.

Despite attempting to limit my exposure to the words used in reporting the story, there are some that are familiar to my own story of surviving 9/11, "running" and "screaming" used to describe the innocent people in the streets running, and screaming, for their lives.

I know that level of terror-driven panic, running to stay alive, caught up in a mental confusion that prohibits rational thinking of where to find safety.

I still remember the running and panic of all of us in the streets the morning of 9/11, scrambling to live as debris rained down on us.

The screams of those around me, which are unlike any other scream.

The only screaming I remember coming from my mouth was in the form of words. It was as I turned right onto Fulton Street, still running.

I screamed, "God, save us all."

I don't know where those specific words came from, because even as I screamed them to the heavens, I knew I was asking for the impossible.

I wonder how many of those running on the street in Nice called out to their God as well.

I will be speaking to over one thousand high school students in September in honor of the fifteenth anniversary of 9/11.

These students are growing up in a world so unlike the one I grew up in.

When I was in high school, I wasn't even aware of the words *terrorism* and *terrorist attack.*

I know bad things happened back then, but we weren't exposed to the resulting images of death and destruction as these students are today. Social media has made that quick access possible.

The students I will be standing in front of are probably accustomed to the words *terrorism* and *terrorist attack* because this is the world they live in.

This is the world post-9/11.

Therefore, I believe it's important for survivors of 9/11 to tell their stories, particularly to students.

This is why I share my own story. Because 9/11 is when everything changed and the world I knew was taken away and replaced with the world where acts of terror seem to happen every week. This is the world these students are growing up in.

We hear of the tragic, traumatic events that become big news stories. What about the ones that we don't hear about? That we are unaware of?

I hope the students I will be speaking to will not grow up living their lives in constant fear, assuming no place is safe. I hope they will venture out into this messed-up world and live their lives.

They might not find answers to stop global terrorism and warped justifications for hate and disregard for human life and dignity, but they hold the possibilities of stopping the cruelty and inhumane regard toward others in our own country.

In response to the massacre in Orlando, the Broadway community came together to record the song "What the World Needs Now," the solution the song suggests being "love, sweet love."

Some may regard that as unrealistic or sugarcoated simplicity. But try loving someone who you look down on as unlovable and you will see how difficult it can be.

I told myself I would never address politics or religion in my writing. Yet it is these two institutions, with a significant majority of people, that have no idea of what projecting and promoting "love, sweet love" looks like.

They know, instead, how to project and promote "hate, pure hate."

They do so using discrimination, inequality, and disparity and "anti" anything that differs from what they think the world should look like.

And in large part due to them, we don't have to look beyond our country to witness atrocities. We can see them within our borders.

We fear for our safety when making travel plans abroad, yet lesbian, gay, bisexual, or transgender students fear for their safety every day of their young lives because of the discrimination, ridicule, and rejection of their parents, peers, teachers, principals, and school administrators.

We fear the possibility of a fanatic with a gun in a crowded venue, yet a person of color fears a bullet each time he or she walks out the front door.

We fear the possibility of a bomb or gunman entering our workplace or school, yet a policeman or -woman begins a shift with the fear of not knowing what he or she might walk into that day.

I wish 9/11 never happened. I wish terrorists weren't still a threat. I wish. I wish. I wish for "love, sweet love. It's the only thing that there's just too little of."

For Mom and Others Who Grieve

If you have lived through just one traumatic event in your life, you can consider yourself extremely fortunate.

Most people experience more than one trauma in a lifetime—life moments they might not even be aware of as traumatic at that time.

I define a traumatic event as something that changes the course of your life as you know it. It also dramatically changes you, no longer being the same person you once were. You are tasked to discover or define what your "new normal" will now look like.

Traumatic events produce within us emotions of grief, fear, anxiety, and isolation, among others.

I have recently experienced a new traumatic event in my life: losing my mother on April 13, 2017. She was eighty-five and had been through so many medical scares, procedures, and hospital stays that I marvel at how she carried on.

But, this time, her illnesses became too strong to fight any longer. And she was being treated, yet again, in the hospital.

I got the phone call from one of her doctors early on a Monday morning to compassionately tell me there was "no more they could do" for my mom. He suggested we now think of palliative care.

Upon waking, my father and I got to the hospital as quickly as we could. We walked into my mom's hospital room, where she had just finished speaking with two ladies from palliative care. My mom told my father and me she had decided it was time for her to stop all these futile medical treatments and turn to hospice.

In the hall, I asked a nurse if we were talking about just a matter of days. She answered yes and that I should call Sue.

Sue arrived early Tuesday morning, and as we gathered in Mom's room, Mom said all she wanted to say. She told us how much she loved each of us.

And we responded in kind. I wasn't rational enough to realize we were really saying our goodbyes. My mind was beginning to go numb.

Those final goodbyes are all I, or my father, can remember. The rest of that day and the days that followed are a blur. I can't remember what we said in my mom's room or what we, the family, talked about among ourselves at home.

My father and I spent the night; he was sleeping in a recliner, me on a cot. The only thing I next remember is being woken at 4:10 a.m. Thursday morning by a nurse who simply said, "She's passed." The nurses came in each hour to check on her, and at 3:00, we were told her heartbeats were slowing down. Both my dad and I question why we didn't stay awake. Why we allowed sleep to overtake us. I can only assume that's what Mom preferred. I hope she knows that we were there by her side. That she wasn't alone.

I went to her, still in her hospital bed, and touched her now-cold hand and caressed her face, just as cold, crying. I put my cheek next to hers, kissed her forehead, and told her how much I loved her.

And now the arrangements that were made are over. The memorial was held. Now my family (from Dad to the great-grandchildren) must discover what our new normal will be without Mom's presence in it.

And I know there is yet at least one other trauma I will face in the future: my dad's passing. And another new normal will then have to be defined.

I realize I have probably written this as my own catharsis, but I also want this to be directed to all readers who have already, or will in their future, live through their own traumatic event(s). Don't let anyone diminish what you go through and what you call it. Losing a beloved family pet can be traumatic. Traumas and tragedies don't all have to be on the same scale as a terrorist attack or a national disaster.

A prolonged illness, a car accident, a broken relationship, being let go from work—remember, anything that changes your life as you knew it can be declared a *trauma*.

And however long it will take for you to find your new normal will be how long it takes. There are no rules or guidelines on how to grieve or begin to heal or attempt to live your life with what you've lost.

Anne Lamott is one of my favorite writers, and she has a quote I love. Her wise words can pertain to the loss of a person or the shattering of a life. It follows.

And I felt like my heart had been so thoroughly and irreparably broken that there could be no real joy again, that at best there might eventually be a little contentment. Everyone wanted me to get help and rejoin life, pick up the pieces and move on, and I tried to, I wanted to, but I just had to lie in the mud with my arms wrapped around myself, eyes closed, grieving until I didn't have to anymore.

Give yourself permission to do just that.

A Weekend of Respite

I can only speak for myself, knowing that my living with PTSD differs from all others' experiences. I live with it as a constant companion. So constant that I'm used to the intrusive thoughts, the flashbacks, the anxiety and depression, the desire to isolate.

But I discovered, a few weeks back, that I could take a respite from all the above. Only for a weekend, but it was a surprising weekend, where there were moments I took pleasure in. Not joy, mind you. That continues to elude me since 9/11. But I found pleasure in the company of good friends, shared memories, and times of genuine laughter.

Five college friends of mine and I had been talking (via Facebook) about getting together for a reunion weekend. One friend graciously offered his beautiful home in the mountains of North Carolina as our gathering place. So, after years of discussing it, we finally planned it, and that is the weekend I speak of where I found respite.

I chose to drive to North Carolina, but instead of driving the straight eight hours it would take, I decided to divide it up and left on a Thursday and drove halfway, staying overnight at a hotel.

There is something about the solitude of driving alone in my car that comforts me. It allows me to think through whatever emotions are present at any given time and, if need be, to express those emotions, be it through tears or a smile that only I am privy to. There were tears during my trip because I experienced a new traumatic event in April: the passing of my mother. A major loss such as that certainly is a tragedy and a trauma. So, as I drove, many of my thoughts centered on my mom and my missing her, weeping as I remembered her. And I did have the intrusion of images of 9/11 (as I do almost daily), which bring their own brand of tears.

But I felt as if I were in the safety of a cocoon while driving in my car with my companion, my service dog, Ranger.

Getting away from home (which was still a home filled with grief) was cathartic for me. So, I could take pleasure in being on the open road. And having driven halfway to North Carolina, I stayed overnight at a nice hotel. There is something about hotels for me. I love staying in them. I could make a vacation out of going from one hotel to another. So, I could enjoy that simple pleasure that night.

I reached my friend's house the next day, and one by one, the others arrived. The house was situated high in the mountains with a spectacular view one could take in from a huge wraparound deck.

As often happens when old friends or acquaintances meet, we all clicked together almost instantly. And as we sat around a fire pit on that grand deck, the stories of catch-up began. I found myself laughing—something I don't do very much of. And I could focus on the moments, while the thoughts that can cause me to freeze up inside stayed far in the back recesses of my mind.

When talking with one of my friends alone, he asked if I'd be open to sharing my story of 9/11 with him and the others later that evening. I'm glad he asked me because it seems people usually shy away from even bringing the subject up. It wouldn't have been upsetting to share my story because 9/11 is a vital chapter in my life. And we were all sharing moments from our pasts; my past contains witnessing and surviving 9/11.

As it turned out, I never did get to tell my story to them. Not this time. The direction of the conversations just didn't segue into it. In fact, I spent a great deal of time that night telling a story about another period of my life, which, for me, serves as a reminder that my life is more than just 9/11. At sixty-four, the book of my life journey contains many chapters. 9/11 is, indeed, one of those chapters, but it also is the first chapter in the second volume of my life, with volume 1 being pre-9/11.

The weekend lasted Friday through Sunday, but it was an experience of feeling like we had been together a week. And I felt like I'd experienced a week of relaxation.

For once, I could let my symptoms of PTSD not rule those three days. Oh, the symptoms were there, but from whomever or whatever, I was given the grace to not let them rule me for that brief time.

This was my experience. I know some of those living with PTSD don't ever get such an experience, yet I would hope they can, at some time, find their own respite, if even for an hour or a day. I've learned that, for myself, I can have moments when the semblance of my life is as close to "normal" as it can be for me. They might be few and far between, but they will always be welcomed.

Yesterday

It happened yesterday—the momentous repercussions of the approaching anniversary of 9/11.

I thought that I was doing so well this year. That my emotions were in check. I had planned my activities to commemorate the day. I'd already spoken, via webcam, to a class in Las Vegas. And I had two more schools I'd be speaking at on the eleventh and the twelfth. I was even being interviewed on the tenth by a student from England for a book he is writing about 9/11 survivors. So, all my ducks seemed in a row.

Yesterday, my dad and I went to a casino—one of the fun things we like to do occasionally—just for the enjoyment of playing blackjack (responsibly, to anyone who might worry). Along with my dad, I had my constant companion, Ranger, my service dog, with me.

When it came time to give Ranger a restroom break, I took him outside. As we walked over to a grassy area, I looked up at the sky (which was a bright blue), and that's when, out of nowhere, it happened. The weight of 9/11, and all it represents for me, came crashing down on me, like a ton of bricks. My mind was flooded with images and emotions. I wanted to shout to the sky, but instead screamed inwardly with anger, "Why did it have to happen?!? And why did I have to be there?!? I don't want to be a survivor! I don't want these memories!!"

I hate that I must live with images, never knowing when they will assault my attention, overpower my thoughts.

I want to be able to go back in time and relive that day without the Twin Towers ever being hit. I want 9/11 to have been just an ordinary day with an extraordinary blue sky.

At that moment, outside the casino, I was filled with anxiety and grief, and I wanted to just cry. But I was in a public place, so I had to put a lid on all that raw emotion and go back inside.

I sat back down at the blackjack table and tried to bring my focus back to the game, even though my mind was flooded with images, my concentration captured by an attack of anxiety, sadness, and grief. It took all my effort to try to keep my attention on the game, but several times, my dad had to say my name because it was my turn and I was lost in thought, my mental state thoroughly distracted by a barrage of flashbacks.

On my left wrist, I wear a rubber wristband that reads, "I am a 9/11 survivor." The woman to my right, a schoolteacher, said to me, "I just read your bracelet. It makes me want to cry." I thought to myself, *Me too*.

Thankfully, my dad and I were ready to stop playing for the day and go to one of the eateries. I just wanted to crumble in a ball and hide away, choosing instead to go through the motions that I was okay. I could feel a headache coming on as my anxiety level was amplifying.

Our order placed, my dad waited for the food while I took Ranger to a table to pour his food into his collapsible bowl. After gobbling it up, and with my dad still waiting for the food, Ranger looked at me, and I started talking to him (which is not out of the ordinary). Sometimes, when I look in his eyes while speaking to him, I think he's understanding, if not the words then the emotions behind them, as if he can see into my soul.

"I'm sad, Ranger," I told him. "Can you help me?" All he could do was just gaze back at me steadily. But it is a comfort for me to be able to pet him and rub his neck or the top of his head. It helps. That plus the fact I took one of my anti-anxiety pills.

Dad came to the table, and we ate. You might wonder, and Dad, if you're reading this, you might want to ask why I didn't speak up and say what I was going through. For one, it's difficult to explain what I'm going through. The words of a survivor's ordeal can seem like a foreign language. If you weren't there on 9/11, it would be difficult for you to understand, because behind a survivor's words are the sounds and images of war. And unless you've been on that battlefield, you just can't imagine the horror. So, Dad, I'm sorry I didn't speak up. It's just at times it's easier to remain silent and let the inner demons of remembrance run their course.

Ironically, when we got back home, I received a private Facebook message from a fellow survivor. She wrote that she was having a bad day and was trying to get through it. She was thinking of how I was doing that day. Kindred spirits, connecting souls. I wrote back that she wasn't alone.

That it was a bad day for me as well. I then realized it was also September 1. Ten more days.

She wrote back to me something I'd never considered before.

"Some people want us to forget so they don't have to remember."

She ended with "I hope sleep is my friend tonight."

I told her I would try to do some writing. And I did. The words above are the result of my efforts.

I hope they help a fellow survivor. I hope they give a non-survivor a bit of insight. And I hope sleep was a friend for my friend that night.

It Begins in August

I toss and turn in bed each night, with a bombardment of thoughts. Some nights, I surrender and take something to quiet my mind and bring sleep. Some nights, I turn on my nightstand lamp, just as I did every night in my apartment in New York for a year after 9/11. It makes me feel safe.

But then comes the morning, and the apprehension and dread of having to go through the motions of another day.

Sadness, my constant companion, deepens, and familiar cycles of depression seem darker, lingering longer than usual. I've learned to mask them, assuming no one will know what's beneath my seemingly happy exterior.

Images of 9/11 appear more frequently, at times inducing tears I wipe away, hoping no one has noticed. There are times when I want to just weep, and the only place to do so is in the privacy of my car.

I become short fused, easily agitated by the slightest irritating situation or annoyance of someone.

I dream more, the most repetitive one taking place pre-9/11, as I try to warn people about what is going to happen. I beg them not to go to work on 9/11, but they ignore me.

That dream symbolizes the utter helplessness I felt during the nightmarish reality the morning of 9/11.

Sometimes, like at work, I become oblivious to my surroundings, and a movie projector switches on in my mind, and I watch, retracing every step I took on 9/11. I'm overcome with anguish because I couldn't, or didn't, do more that morning. I'm angry that I let self-preservation overcome risking my life to run to the people I watched hitting the ground. I question why I didn't die and find myself teetering on a fine line of imagining if I had and wishing that I had.

I am not alone, though. Every survivor, first responder, rescue and recovery worker, and volunteer in my 9/11 support group faces August similarly. They understand every word, feeling, and emotion I express. We keep the dialogue among ourselves, instead of trying to talk to friends or family, because of the reactions they give, or we assume they will give.

"But you survived. You're alive."

Yes, we walked away from Ground Zero physically alive. But our spirits, the heart of who we were before 9/11, did not survive. That part of us died and can't be restored. Our souls were fractured, and we know they can't be mended. Parts of our soul and spirit were buried among the rubble of the fallen towers.

"You should be over this by now!"

We were ordinary people that day, in the towers, the surrounding buildings, on the streets. And the first responders, fire crews, and police were skilled professionals who, up until that day, thought they had seen it all. All of us, the ordinary and the skilled, were subjected to an unprecedented cataclysmic event none of us could have ever been prepared for.

Carnage ... destruction and devastation ... smoke ... smells ... casualties ... falling debris ... running for our lives ... moments we thought our lives were ending.

We were in a battle zone, surrounded by inconceivable horror.

Most of us are still living in the shadow of post-traumatic stress.

Tell me how we're supposed to get over this.

"Don't dwell on the past. Just move on."

Moments in everyone's past, be they good or bad, contribute to who we become. I am not negating the traumas and tragedies and losses that others face that are unrelated to 9/11. And I wouldn't dare suggest our suffering is of greater importance than others'.

But it is different.

That difference being that the survivors of 9/11 experienced, in that one specific morning, *obliteration*, a word that means to remove or destroy all traces of, do away with, destroy completely.

All traces of who we were on September 10, 2001, were destroyed and done away with. Our lives, as we then knew them, were removed and destroyed completely.

If you tell me I need to move on, you're asking me to put that day in a box and put it away, never to look at it again. You're telling me to forget. I can't do that. No survivor I know can.

9/11 is forever a part of who we are. It is in us, linked to our DNA. That day, we breathed in the smoke and smells. We heard the continuous wail of sirens and screams of people. We saw the casualties of war, the dying and the dead. We felt the pavement if we fell; the debris, as it rained down on us; our tears as they streamed down our faces; the embrace of someone we may not even have known. As we wept together, we felt the skin and blood of the injured we helped. We tasted the ashes from buildings and individuals engulfed in flames.

Therefore, I can't just move on.

But what I can do is try to move forward.

9/11 is in my past. That can't change.

I don't remember what it feels like to be truly happy. This is my present.

Will I ever feel utter joy, happiness, and genuine laughter again? That is my uncertain future.

And I can only have a future if I move forward, one day at a time. Some days I can. Some days I can't.

I still think of 9/11 every day.

I'm not writing to elicit sympathy or pity. I'm writing for the survivors, first responders, rescue and recovery workers, and volunteers who haven't found the words to describe all that stays within.

For most, 9/11 is a part of our country's history, a chapter in the history books. For some, it's as if it happened last week.

And Then My Dad Died

My mother had died in April, and it would be our first Thanksgiving without her sitting at the table, one of the major "firsts" you face when someone you love passes on. None of us was looking forward to it. In fact, I told my dad I'd much rather he and I just go to the casino (where we'd go once a month) than go through the big Thanksgiving fuss and family obligation of us all having to be together. But, knowing this was something we'd have to deal with each Thanksgiving, and the fact that it would help my dad if he were with all the family, I knew we'd have to go to Sue's for the Thanksgiving meal. I knew it would probably help me as well.

Dad and I drove down to Sue's early Thanksgiving morning. When we got there, she was just beginning the preparations; already, the smell of a turkey cooking permeated the house. My niece and nephew and their respective spouses, along with my two great-nieces and three great-nephews, were there. Children are always a comforting balm in such a situation.

We used to gather each year at our parents' home for Thanksgiving and Christmas, with Mom doing the cooking. I'd love waking up those mornings, being greeted by the smells coming from the kitchen. But as the years went by, making the dinners became more of a hardship than Mom could handle, being wheelchair bound. I'm sure it was with a heavy heart she finally said she just couldn't do it anymore. That's when we started going to my Sue's on each of those holidays.

We tried to make this Thanksgiving, minus our matriarch, an enjoyable one. I know my thoughts centered on the absence of Mom. We talked about her with anecdotes of how particular she was each Thanksgiving when she was in charge.

When all the food was finally ready, the turkey and all the trimmings, it was a few minutes of chaos as we set the adults' and children's tables. Dishes were put on the kitchen table buffet style, and we each made our plates and took them into the dining room. It all seemed rushed and scattered since there were so many of us preparing our plates. The first of us to sit at the dining table began to eat while the others made their way in from the kitchen. We had skipped saying a prayer. I think Sue mentioned it. I know, for me, if we prayed, we'd have to address the absence of Mom and pray for her. That was something I wasn't prepared to do, as I assume was the case for everyone else.

Dad seemed to be in good spirits and full of energy, and he had a healthy appetite. After we ate, he enjoyed coloring with his great-grandchildren. Once everyone left, it was just Dad and me and my sister and brother-in-law. It was early in the evening when he began to complain of a slight stomachache. We chalked it up to him perhaps eating too much. But as the evening progressed, the ache became a sharp pain, and then Dad said the pain was excruciating. He went to lie down, and about eleven o'clock that night, he asked us to call an ambulance. That indicated to us that, for him to ask for us to call 911, he had to be ill.

By the time the ambulance arrived, he was doubled over with pain. Sue was hysterically crying as he was taken out of the house on a stretcher. I was used to calling 911 over the past six years living with my folks. They both had so many emergency health issues, and it felt like one of them would be in the hospital at any given time. But, this was all new for my sister.

Once in the emergency room, they gave him morphine for his pain and started running a battery of tests. They couldn't give us a definitive diagnosis that night, so they admitted him into the hospital. Nine days later, he died. They found that his gallbladder was filled with infection. Ideally, it should have been taken out, but Dad was too high of a risk to have the surgery. Instead, a tube was inserted into the gallbladder to drain the infection. In a matter of days, his kidneys began to fail him, and then he developed pneumonia.

The Saturday after Thanksgiving, December 3, Sue and I were with him during the day. At one point, he told us that he was sorry, but he was going to leave us to go be with our mom. Not wanting to believe he was that sick, I asked him, "When are you going?" and he replied, "Tuesday." I just assumed it was the ramblings caused by the pain medications he was on.

Sue and I left the hospital late in the afternoon. It was early evening, and we were watching TV when my cell phone rang. It was Dad, and he asked, almost belligerently, where I was. In response, I told him I was at Sue's. I was bewildered by why he wouldn't have known that. He then told me I had better get there (the hospital) because they were trying to make him perform in a play and he didn't want to. I asked him who "they" were and he, obviously now delusional, never answered the question. He was just insisting that I get there because they wanted him to perform in *Brokeback Mountain* and he didn't want to do it. Even though his apparent mental state was cause for alarm, I was surprised that he even knew about that movie. Why he named that film was baffling. I told him Sue and I would be right over, and we left immediately to get to the hospital.

When we walked into his room, he was still agitated and adamant that the elusive "they" were trying to get him to perform the play and that all we had to do was wait and we'd see that he was right. We never did find out what the cause was behind his irrational lapse in thinking coherently. I assured him that no one could make him do anything while we were there. Sue and I decided we would spend the night in his room.

Once Dad calmed down a bit, he fell into a deep sleep. Sue and I sat and watched him sleep. I focused on the rhythm of his stomach rising as he took each breath.

His bed was in a reclining position, and later that night, his head was at an odd angle on the pillow, so I went to the side of his bed and gingerly repositioned it, moving his pillow to give him more support. I stood there, looking down at him. Suddenly, while still asleep, he made a sound that is difficult to describe. A combination of gurgling and choking, his tongue protruding through his open mouth. Sue ran out of the room to get a nurse, and in the few seconds she was out in the hall, I watched my father take what was to be his final breath. His stomach was no longer rising. I felt for a pulse. Before the nurse came in, Dad died with me by his side.

Within a matter of minutes, I went from having a living parent to being parentless—a life-altering event that has changed me forever. I now mourn the loss of both my dad and my mom and learn to adjust to a life without their presence.

Unlike 9/11, I knew the day would come when my parents would no longer be with me, so it wasn't a catastrophic event. But it was traumatic nonetheless, especially having a parent pass as you are standing next to him.

A traumatic event changes a person. After living through even a moment of tragedy, your life will, from that point on, be defined not by who you were before the trauma but by who you are now since having lived through an unforgettable ordeal. Traumatic events shape our perception of ourselves, our beliefs, and our questioning of our place in this world.

Epilogue

I want it to go away. I don't want it to have happened.

But it won't, and it did, and I was there.

I wanted to catch that falling man with the flailing arms and legs.

But I couldn't, and I didn't, though I was there.

I wanted to be a hero, doing more than I humanly could.

But I wasn't, and I didn't.

I wanted to stay there, in the street, not afraid.

But I didn't, and I was.

I wanted to be there through the end.

But I wasn't.

I wanted to stay and rescue.

But I didn't.

I wanted to be more injured, dirtier, more at risk.

But I wasn't.

I want to imagine being buried, being missing, being gone.

But I can't.

I want to know why I survived and others didn't.

But I don't.

I want it never to have happened.

But it did.